McDougal Littell
Pre-Algebra

Larson   Boswell   Kanold   Stiff

Notetaking Guide

The Notetaking Guide contains a lesson-by-lesson framework that allows students to take notes on and review the main concepts of each lesson in the textbook. Each Notetaking Guide lesson features worked-out examples and Checkpoint exercises similar to those found in the textbook. Each example has a number of write-in boxes for students to complete, either in class as the example is discussed or at home as part of a review of the lesson. Each chapter concludes with a review of the main vocabulary of the chapter. Upon completion, each chapter of the Notetaking Guide can be used by students to help review for the test on that particular chapter.

McDougal Littell
A DIVISION OF HOUGHTON MIFFLIN COMPANY
Evanston, Illinois   •   Boston   •   Dallas

ISBN-13: 978-0-618-25657-0   ISBN-10: 0-618-25657-1

14 15 16 17 0928 13 12 11 10

Contents

Contents

Contents

Contents

1.1 Expressions and Variables

Goal: Evaluate and write variable expressions.

Vocabulary

Numerical expression:

Variable:

Variable expression:

Evaluate a variable expression:

Verbal model:

Example 1 *Evaluating a Variable Expression*

Evaluate the expression $3 \cdot b$ when $b = 90$.

Solution

$3 \cdot b = 3 \cdot \boxed{}$ Substitute for b.

$= \boxed{}$ Multiply.

> When you write a variable expression involving multiplication, avoid using the symbol $\times$. It may be confused with the variable x.

Example 2 *Evaluating Expressions with Two Variables*

Evaluate the expression when $x = 9$ and $y = 5$.

a. $x + y = \boxed{} + \boxed{}$ Substitute for x and for y.

$= \boxed{}$ Add.

b. $xy = \boxed{}\left(\boxed{}\right)$ Substitute for x and for y.

$= \boxed{}$ Multiply.

✔ Checkpoint Evaluate the expression when $x = 8$ and $y = 2$.

1. $x + 12$	2. $x - y$	3. $\dfrac{x}{y}$

Common Words and Phrases that Indicate Operations

Addition	Subtraction	Multiplication	Division
plus	minus	times	divided by
the sum of	the difference of	the product of	divided into
increased by	decreased by	multiplied by	the quotient of
total	fewer than	of	
more than	less than		
added to	subtracted from		

Example 3 *Writing a Variable Expression*

Editing You have a 350-page manuscript that needs to be edited very quickly. You are going to divide the number of pages among several editors. You want to give the same number of pages to each editor. Use a verbal model to write a variable expression for the number of pages given to each editor if you know the number of editors.

Solution

Let e represent the number of editors. The phrase *divide* indicates

[   ]

Number of pages for each editor	=	Total number of pages	÷	[ ]

| | = | [   ] | ÷ | [   ] |

Answer: The number of pages for each editor is [   ] ÷ [   ],

or [   ].

> When you write a variable expression involving division, use a fraction bar instead of the division symbol ÷. For example, write the "quotient of n and 12" as $\dfrac{n}{12}$.

1.2 Powers and Exponents

Goal: Use powers to describe repeated multiplication.

Vocabulary

Power:

Base:

Exponent:

Formula:

Example 1   Using Exponents

Write the product using an exponent.

a. $7 \cdot 7 \cdot 7 \cdot 7 \cdot 7 = 7^{\boxed{}}$ The base $\boxed{}$ is used as a factor $\boxed{}$ times.

b. $(0.4)(0.4) = (0.4)^{\boxed{}}$ The base $\boxed{}$ is used as a factor $\boxed{}$ times.

c. $a \cdot a \cdot a \cdot a = a^{\boxed{}}$ The base $\boxed{}$ is used as a factor $\boxed{}$ times.

d. $r \cdot r \cdot r \cdot r \cdot r \cdot r = r^{\boxed{}}$ The base $\boxed{}$ is used as a factor $\boxed{}$ times.

✔ **Checkpoint** Write the product using an exponent.

1. $12 \cdot 12 \cdot 12 \cdot 12$	2. $(0.2)(0.2)(0.2)(0.2)(0.2)(0.2)(0.2)$
3. $x \cdot x \cdot x \cdot x \cdot x$	4. $y \cdot y \cdot y$

Example 2 — Evaluating Powers with Variables

Evaluate the expression x^3 when $x = 0.4$.

$x^3 = \left(\boxed{}\right)^3$ Substitute for x.

$= \left(\boxed{}\right)\left(\boxed{}\right)\left(\boxed{}\right)$ Use $\boxed{}$ as a factor $\boxed{}$ times.

$= \boxed{}$ Multiply.

Area and Volume Formulas

> Area is measured in square units, such as square feet (ft^2) or square centimeters (cm^2). Volume is measured in cubic units, such as cubic inches (in.^3) or cubic meters (m^3).

Area A of a square

$$A = s^2$$

Volume V of a cube

$$V = s^3$$

Example 3 — Using Powers in Formulas

Room Size You are planning to put wall-to-wall carpeting in your room. To do this, you need to find the area of the square-shaped floor.

11 ft

11 ft

Solution

$A = s^2$ Write the formula.

$= \left(\boxed{}\right)^2$ Substitute for s.

$= \boxed{}$ Evaluate power.

Answer: The area of the floor is $\boxed{}$ square feet.

✔ **Checkpoint**   Evaluate the expression when $n = 2$.

5. n^2	6. n^3	7. n^4	8. n^5

Find the volume of a cube with the given side length.

9. 2 meters	10. 3 feet

Order of Operations

Goal: Use order of operations to evaluate expressions.

Vocabulary

Order of
operations:

Grouping
symbols:

Order of Operations

1. Evaluate expressions inside grouping symbols.

2. Evaluate powers.

3. Multiply and divide from left to right.

4. Add and subtract from left to right.

Example 1   *Using Order of Operations*

Evaluate the expression 4 · 20 + 8 · 5 + 4.8.

$4 \cdot 20 + 8 \cdot 5 + 4.8$ Write expression.

$= \boxed{} + \boxed{} + 4.8$ Multiply.

$= \boxed{}$ Add.

✓ *Checkpoint* **Evaluate the expression.**

1. $25 - 6 \cdot 3$	**2.** $56 \div 8 - 4$

Example 2   *Using Grouping Symbols*

Evaluate the expression.

a. $5(14 - 3.8) = 5\left(\boxed{}\right)$ Subtract within parentheses.

$ = \boxed{}$ Multiply.

b. $\dfrac{27 - 3}{4 + 2} = \left(\boxed{}\right) \div \left(\boxed{}\right)$ Rewrite fraction as division.

$\phantom{\dfrac{27-3}{4+2}} = \boxed{} \div \boxed{}$ Evaluate within parentheses.

$\phantom{\dfrac{27-3}{4+2}} = \boxed{}$ Divide.

c. $4 \cdot [35 - (11 + 8)] = 4 \cdot \left[35 - \boxed{}\right]$ Add within parentheses.

$ = 4 \cdot \boxed{}$ Subtract within brackets.

$ = \boxed{}$ Multiply.

> When grouping symbols appear inside other grouping symbols, work from the innermost grouping symbols out.

Example 3   *Evaluating Variable Expressions*

Evaluate the expression when $x = 3$ and $y = 6$.

a. $3(x + y) = 3\left(\boxed{} + \boxed{}\right)$ Substitute for x and for y.

$ = 3\left(\boxed{}\right)$ Add within parentheses.

$ = \boxed{}$ Multiply.

b. $5(y - x)^2 = 5\left(\boxed{} - \boxed{}\right)^2$ Substitute for x and for y.

$ = 5\left(\boxed{}\right)^2$ Subtract within parentheses.

$ = 5\left(\boxed{}\right)$ Evaluate power.

$ = \boxed{}$ Multiply.

✓ **Checkpoint** **Evaluate the expression when $x = 4$ and $y = 5$.**

3. $y(19 - x^2)$	4. $\dfrac{6y}{x + 1}$

1.4 Comparing and Ordering Integers

Goal: Compare and order integers.

Vocabulary

Integers:

Negative integers:

Positive integers:

Absolute Value:

Opposites:

> The expression −a is always read as "the opposite of a" and *not* as "negative a." If *a* is a positive number, then −a is a negative number. If *a* is a negative number, then −a is a positive number.

Example 1   *Graphing and Ordering Integers*

Use a number line to order these integers from least to greatest: 0, −6, −2, −8, 7, −9, 3.

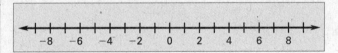

Read the numbers from left to right:  ☐, ☐, ☐, ☐, ☐, ☐, ☐.

✓ *Checkpoint* **Graph the integers on a number line. Then write the integers in order from least to greatest.**

1. 2, −7, 6, 4, 0, −4, −1

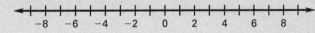

Example 2   *Finding Absolute Value*

State the absolute value of the number.

a. 7   b. −5

Solution

a.

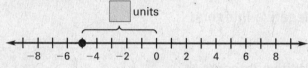

The distance between 7 and ☐ is ☐. So, $|7| = $ ☐.

b.

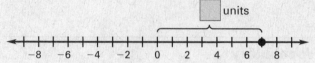

The distance between −5 and ☐ is ☐. So, $|-5| = $ ☐.

Example 3   *Finding Opposites*

State the opposite of the number.

a. 3   b. −8

Solution

a.

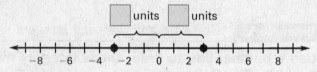

The opposite of 3 is ☐.

b.

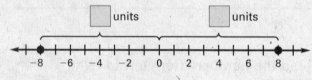

The opposite of −8 is ☐.

✓ **Checkpoint**   **State the absolute value and the opposite of the number.**

2. 9	3. −12

1.5 Adding Integers

Goal: Add integers.

Vocabulary

Additive inverse:

Additive inverse property:

Example 1 *Adding Integers Using a Number Line*

Use a number line to find the sum.

a. $7 + (-10)$

Start at ⬚. Then move ⬚ units to the ⬚.

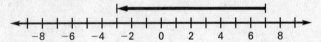

Answer: The final position is ⬚. So, $7 + (-10) = $ ⬚.

b. $-6 + 5$

Start at ⬚. Then move ⬚ units to the ⬚.

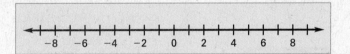

Answer: The final position is ⬚. So, $-6 + 5 = $ ⬚.

✓ **Checkpoint** Use a number line to find the sum.

1. $9 + (-6)$	2. $-2 + (-6)$
–10 –8 –6 –4 –2 0 2 4 6 8 10	–10 –8 –6 –4 –2 0 2 4 6 8 10

Adding Integers

Words | **Numbers**

1. **Same Sign** Add the absolute values and use the [   ]. | $8 + 12 = $ [   ]
$-6 + (-4) = $ [   ]

2. **Different Signs** Subtract the [   ] absolute value from the [   ] absolute value and use the sign of the number with the [   ] absolute value. | $5 + (-8) = $ [   ]
$-11 + 13 = $ [ ]

3. **Opposites** The sum of a number and its opposite is [ ]. | $7 + (-7) = $ [ ]

Example 2 *Adding Two Integers*

a. $-35 + (-18) = $ [   ]

Same sign: Add | [   ] | and | [   ] |.

Both integers are [   ], so the sum is [   ].

b. $27 + (-13) = $ [   ]

Different signs: Subtract | [   ] | from | [ ] |.

Because | [   ] | > | [   ] |, the sum has the same sign as [ ].

Example 3 *Adding More Than Two Integers*

Find the sum $-7 + (-41) + 32$.

$-7 + (-41) + 32 = $ [   ] $+ 32$ Add -7 and -41.

$= $ [   ]   Add [   ] and 32.

✓ *Checkpoint* **Find the sum.**

3. $-19 + 36$	4. $-29 + (-31) + 47$

1.6 Subtracting Integers

Goal: Subtract integers.

Subtracting Integers

Words To subtract an integer, add its [   ].

Numbers $3 - 7 = 3 + ($ [   ] $) = $ [   ]

Algebra $a - b = a + ($ [   ] $)$

Example 1 *Subtracting Integers*

a. $5 - 9 = 5 + ($ [   ] $)$

$= $ [   ]

b. $3 - (-8) = 3 + $ [   ]

$= $ [   ]

c. $-4 - (-10) = -4 + $ [   ]

$= $ [   ]

To subtract 9, add its opposite, [   ].

Add 5 and [   ].

To subtract -8, add its opposite, [   ].

Add 3 and [   ].

To subtract -10, add its opposite, [   ].

Add -4 and [   ].

✔ **Checkpoint** **Find the difference.**

1. $3 - 8$	2. $-2 - 9$	3. $6 - (-3)$

Example 2   *Evaluating Variable Expressions*

Evaluate the expression when x = −8.

a. $x - (-22) = \boxed{} - (-22)$ Substitute for x.

$\qquad\qquad = \boxed{} + \boxed{}$ To subtract −22, add $\boxed{}$.

$\qquad\qquad = \boxed{}$ Add $\boxed{}$ and $\boxed{}$.

b. $9 - x = 9 - \left(\boxed{}\right)$ Substitute for x.

$\qquad\quad = 9 + \boxed{}$ To subtract $\boxed{}$, add $\boxed{}$.

$\qquad\quad = \boxed{}$ Add 9 and $\boxed{}$.

✔ *Checkpoint*   **Evaluate the expression when y = −12.**

4. y − 6	**5.** 19 − y	**6.** −7 − y

Example 3   *Evaluating Change*

Write a verbal model to find the change in temperature given the start temperature and the end temperature. Use the model to find the change in temperature from −5°F to 12°F.

Solution

> You can use subtraction to find the change in a variable quantity such as elevation or temperature. Subtract the original value of the quantity from the value after the change.

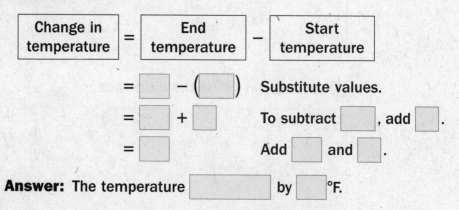

Change in temperature	=	End temperature	−	Start temperature

$\qquad\qquad\quad = \boxed{} - \left(\boxed{}\right)$ Substitute values.

$\qquad\qquad\quad = \boxed{} + \boxed{}$ To subtract $\boxed{}$, add $\boxed{}$.

$\qquad\qquad\quad = \boxed{}$ Add $\boxed{}$ and $\boxed{}$.

Answer: The temperature $\boxed{}$ by $\boxed{}$ °F.

✔ *Checkpoint*   **Find the change in temperature.**

7. From −3°F to 8°F	**8.** From −15°C to −2°C

Multiplying and Dividing Integers

Goal: Multiply and divide integers.

Multiplying Integers

Words   **Numbers**

The product of two integers with [ ] sign is [ ]. $2(4) = $ [ ] $-2(-4) = $ [ ]

The product of two integers with [ ] signs is [ ]. $2(-4) = $ [ ] $-2(4) = $ [ ]

The product of any integer and 0 is [ ]. $2(0) = $ [ ] $-2(0) = $ [ ]

Example 1   *Multiplying Integers*

a. $-5(-8) = $ [ ]   Same sign: Product is [ ].

b. $-8(7) = $ [ ]   Different signs: Product is [ ].

c. $-51(0) = $ [ ]   The product of any integer and 0 is [ ].

✓ **Checkpoint**   Find the product.

1. $7(-12)$	**2.** $-9(-5)$
3. $-250(0)$	**4.** $-4(11)$

Dividing Integers

Words	Numbers
The quotient of two integers with ⬚⬚⬚ sign is ⬚⬚⬚.	$8 \div 4 = \boxed{}$ $-8 \div (-4) = \boxed{}$
The quotient of two integers with ⬚⬚⬚ signs is ⬚⬚⬚.	$-8 \div 4 = \boxed{}$ $8 \div (-4) = \boxed{}$
The quotient of 0 and any nonzero integer is ⬚.	$0 \div 4 = \boxed{}$ $0 \div (-4) = \boxed{}$

Example 2   *Dividing Integers*

a. $-63 \div (-9) = \boxed{}$ Same sign: Quotient is ⬚⬚⬚.

b. $24 \div (-4) = \boxed{}$ Different signs: Quotient is ⬚⬚⬚.

c. $0 \div (-2) = \boxed{}$ The quotient of 0 and any nonzero integer is ⬚.

✔ *Checkpoint*   Find the quotient.

5. $0 \div (-43)$	**6.** $32 \div (-4)$
7. $-28 \div 7$	**8.** $-38 \div (-19)$

1.8 The Coordinate Plane

Goal: Identify and plot points in a coordinate plane.

Vocabulary

Coordinate plane:

x-axis:

y-axis:

Origin:

Quadrant:

Ordered pair:

x-coordinate:

y-coordinate:

Scatter plot:

Example 1 *Naming Points in a Coordinate Plane*

Give the coordinates of the point.

a. *A*   **b.** *B*

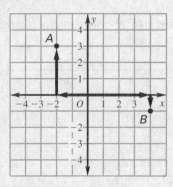

Solution

a. Point *A* is ☐ units to the ☐ of the origin and ☐ units ☐.
The *x*-coordinate is ☐ and the *y*-coordinate is ☐. The
coordinates are (☐, ☐).

b. Point *B* is ☐ units to the ☐ of the origin and ☐ unit
☐. The *x*-coordinate is ☐ and the *y*-coordinate is ☐.
The coordinates are (☐, ☐).

✔ *Checkpoint* **Give the coordinates of the point.**

1. *C*

2. *D*

3. *E*

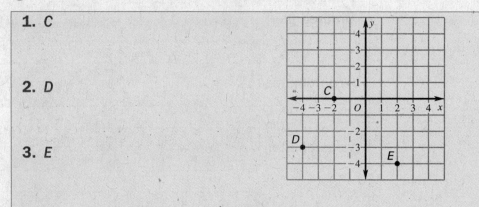

Example 2 | *Plotting Points in a Coordinate Plane*

Plot the point in the coordinate plane. Describe the location of the point.

a. $A(2, 3)$ **b.** $B(-4, 0)$ **c.** $C(1, -3)$

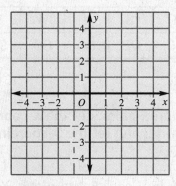

Solution

a. Begin at the origin and move ☐ units to the ☐, then move ☐ units ☐. Point *A* is located ☐.

b. Begin at the origin and move ☐ units to the ☐. Point *B* is located ☐.

c. Begin at the origin and move ☐ unit to the ☐, then move ☐ units ☐. Point *C* is located ☐.

✓ **Checkpoint** Plot the point in the coordinate plane. Describe the location of the point.

4. $D(0, 3)$

5. $E(-2, -4)$

6. $F(-1, 2)$

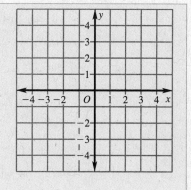

Example 3   *Making a Scatter Plot*

The number of hours you spent studying for 5 different math tests and the score you got on each test is given in the table. Make a scatter plot of the data and describe any relationship you see.

Hours studying	1	3	4	4	5
Test score	55	78	86	89	98

Solution

1. Write the data as ordered pairs. Let the *x*-coordinate represent the hours spent studying, and let the *y*-coordinate represent the test score: ▯.

2. Plot the ordered pairs in a coordinate plane. You need only the first quadrant.

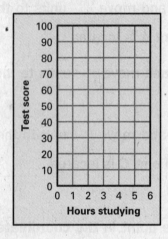

Notice that the points ▯ from left to right. You can conclude as the hours spent studying ▯, your test scores ▯.

Words to Review

Give an example of the vocabulary word.

Numerical expression

Variable

Variable expression

Evaluate a variable expression

Verbal model

Power

Base

Exponent

Integer

Negative integer

Positive integer

Absolute value

Opposite

Additive inverse

Additive inverse property

Coordinate plane, *x*-axis, *y*-axis, origin, quadrant

Ordered pair

***x*-coordinate**

***y*-coordinate**

Scatter plot

Review your notes and Chapter 1 by using the Chapter Review on pages 52–55 of your textbook.

Properties and Operations

Goal: Use properties of addition and multiplication.

Commutative and Associative Properties	
Commutative Property of Addition **Words** In a sum, you can add the numbers in any order. **Numbers** $4 + (-7) = -7 + 4$ **Algebra** $a + b = b + a$	**Commutative Property of Multiplication** **Words** In a product, you can multiply the numbers in any order. **Numbers** $8(-5) = -5(8)$ **Algebra** $ab = ba$
Associative Property of Addition **Words** Changing the grouping of the numbers in a sum does not change the sum. **Numbers** $(9 + 6) + 2 = 9 + (6 + 2)$ **Algebra** $(a + b) + c = a + (b + c)$	**Associative Property of Multiplication** **Words** Changing the grouping of the numbers in a product does not change the product. **Numbers** $(3 \cdot 10) \cdot 4 = 3 \cdot (10 \cdot 4)$ **Algebra** $(a \cdot b) \cdot c = a \cdot (b \cdot c)$

Example 1 *Using Properties of Addition*

Distance This week, you rode in a car for 42 miles, rode a bike for 5 miles, and rode in a bus for 23 miles. Find the total distance.

Solution

The total distance is the sum of the three distances.

> Use properties of addition to group together distances that are easy to add mentally.

$42 + 5 + 23 = (42 + 5) + 23$ Use order of operations.

$ = (\square + \square) + 23$ Commutative property of addition

$ = \square + (\square + 23)$ Associative property of addition

$ = \square + \square$ Add $\square$ and $\square$.

$ = \square$ Add $\square$ and $\square$.

Answer: The total distance is $\square$ miles.

Example 2 *Using Properties of Multiplication*

Evaluate 4*xy* when *x* = −8 and *y* = 15.

$4xy = 4()()$ Substitute for *x* and for *y*.

$= [4()]()$ Use order of operations.

$= [()]()$ Commutative property of multiplication

$= [()()]$ Associative property of multiplication

$= ()$ Multiply ☐ and ☐.

$= $ Multiply ☐ and ☐.

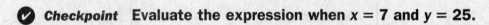 **Checkpoint** Evaluate the expression when *x* = 7 and *y* = 25.

1. $(2x + y) + 46$	**2.** $4x^2y$

Example 3 *Using Properties to Simplify Variable Expressions*

Simplify the expression.

a. $x + 5 + 2 = (x + 5) + 2$ Use order of operations.

$= x + (5 + 2)$ ▭ property of addition

$= x + $ Add 5 and 2.

b. $3(9y) = (3 \cdot 9)y$ ▭ property of multiplication

$= $ Multiply 3 and 9.

 Checkpoint Simplify the expression.

3. $n + 6 + 7$	**4.** $(4r)(-3)$

Identity Properties	
Identity Property of Addition	**Identity Property of Multiplication**
Words The sum of a number and the **additive identity**, 0, is the number.	**Words** The product of a number and the **multiplicative identity**, 1, is the number.
Numbers $-6 + 0 = -6$	**Numbers** $4 \cdot 1 = 4$
Algebra $a + 0 = a$	**Algebra** $a \cdot 1 = a$

Example 4 *Identifying Properties*

Statement	Property Illustrated
a. $(3 + 2) + 4 = 3 + (2 + 4)$	
b. $0 + b = b$	
c. $1(-7) = -7$	
d. $cd = dc$	

✔ **Checkpoint** **Identify the property that the statement illustrates.**

5. $(2 \cdot 6) \cdot 3 = 2 \cdot (6 \cdot 3)$	6. $q + (-r) = -r + q$

2.2 The Distributive Property

Goal: Use the distributive property.

Vocabulary

Equivalent numerical expressions:

Equivalent variable expressions:

The Distributive Property

Algebra $a(b + c) = ab + ac$

$(b + c)a = ba + ca$

$a(b - c) = ab - ac$

$(b - c)a = ba - ca$

Numbers $4(6 + 3) = $

$(6 + 3)4 = $

$5(7 - 2) = $

$(7 - 2)5 = $

Example 1 *Using the Distributive Property*

Crafts You are buying beads for a craft project. You need gold, silver, and white beads. A bag of each type of bead costs $3.99. Use the distributive property and mental math to find the total cost of the beads.

Solution

Total cost = 3(3.99)　　　　Write expression for total cost.

$= 3(\boxed{} - \boxed{})$　　Rewrite 3.99 as $\boxed{} - \boxed{}$.

$= 3(\boxed{}) - 3(\boxed{})$　　Distributive property

$= \boxed{} - \boxed{}$　　Multiply using mental math.

$= \boxed{}$　　Subtract using mental math.

Answer: The total cost of the beads is $\boxed{}$.

✔ **Checkpoint** Use the distributive property to evaluate the expression.

1. $2(9 + 4)$	**2.** $(12 - 3)3$	**3.** $(4 - 11)(-4)$

Evaluate the expression using the distributive property and mental math.

4. $5(103)$	**5.** $4(3.8)$	**6.** $3(6.03)$

Example 2   *Writing Equivalent Variable Expressions*

Use the distributive property to write an equivalent variable expression.

a. $2(x + 10) = $ ⬚   Distributive property

$= $ ⬚   Multiply.

b. $(m + 3)(-4) = $ ⬚   Distributive property

$= $ ⬚   Multiply.

$= $ ⬚   Definition of subtraction

c. $-3(2y - 6) = $ ⬚   Distributive property

$= $ ⬚   Multiply.

$= $ ⬚   Definition of subtraction

7. $(x + 7)4$	**8.** $-3(4m - 7)$

Example 3   *Finding Areas of Geometric Figures*

Find the area of the rectangle or triangle.

a.

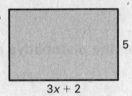

5

$3x + 2$

b.

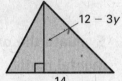

$12 - 3y$

14

Solution

a. Use the formula for the area of a rectangle.

$A = \ell w$

$= (\quad\quad)(\quad)$

$= \boxed{\ }(\boxed{\ }) + \boxed{\ }(\boxed{\ })$

$= \boxed{\qquad}$

Answer: The area is $\boxed{\qquad}$ square units.

b. Use the formula for the area of a triangle.

$A = \frac{1}{2}bh = \frac{1}{2}(\quad\quad)(\quad\quad)$

$= \boxed{\ }(\quad\quad)$

$= \boxed{\ }(\quad) - \boxed{\ }(\quad)$

$= \boxed{\qquad}$

Answer: The area is $\boxed{\qquad}$ square units.

✔ **Checkpoint**   Find the area of the rectangle or triangle.

9.

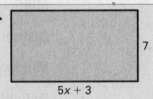

7

$5x + 3$

10.

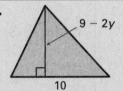

$9 - 2y$

10

Simplifying Variable Expressions

Goal: Simplify variable expressions.

Vocabulary

Terms of an expression:

Coefficient of a term:

Constant term:

Like terms:

Example 1 *Identifying Parts of an Expression*

Identify the terms, like terms, coefficients, and constant terms of the expression $5 - 2x - 3 + x$.

Solution

1. Write the expression as a sum:

2. Identify the parts of the expression. Note that because $x = \boxed{}\,x$, the coefficient of x is $\boxed{}$.

   Terms: **Like terms:**

   Coefficients: **Constant terms:**

✔ **Checkpoint** Identify the terms, like terms, coefficients, and constant terms of the expression.

1. $4y - 6 + 3y$	2. $9 + w - 5 - 8w$

Example 2   *Simplifying an Expression*

$5m + 8 - 3m - 7 = 5m + 8 + \left(\boxed{} \right) + \left(\boxed{} \right)$ Write as a sum.

$= 5m + \left(\boxed{} \right) + \boxed{} + \left(\boxed{} \right)$ Commutative property

$= \left[\boxed{} + \left(\boxed{} \right) \right]m + \boxed{} + \left(\boxed{} \right)$ Distributive property

$= \boxed{}$ Simplify.

Example 3   *Simplifying Expressions with Parentheses*

a. $3(x + 2) - x + 9 = \boxed{} - x + 9$ Distributive property

$= \boxed{}$ Group like terms.

$= \boxed{}$ Combine like terms.

b. $2k - 5(k + 4) = 2k - \boxed{}$ Distributive property

$= \boxed{}$ Combine like terms.

c. $5a - (5a - 7) = 5a - \boxed{}(5a - 7)$ Identity property

$= 5a - \boxed{}$ Distributive property

$= \boxed{}$ Combine like terms.

$= \boxed{}$ Simplify.

✔ **Checkpoint**   Simplify the expression.

3. $4y - 6 + 3y$	**4.** $9 + w - 5 - 8w$
5. $4(x - 1) - 2x - 7$	**6.** $-6(k + 3) + 5k$

2.4 Variables and Equations

Goal: Solve equations with variables.

Vocabulary

Equation:

Solution of an equation:

Solving an equation:

Example 1 — *Writing Verbal Sentences as Equations*

Verbal Sentence	Equation
a. The sum of x and 4 is 8.	
b. The difference of 7 and y is 13.	
c. The product of -2 and p is 24.	
d. The quotient of n and 3 is 5.	

Example 2 — *Checking Possible Solutions*

Tell whether 7 or 8 is a solution of $x - 3 = 5$.

a. Substitute 7 for x.

$$x - 3 = 5$$
$$\boxed{} - 3 \overset{?}{=} 5$$
$$\boxed{}\ \boxed{}\ 5$$

Answer: 7 $\boxed{}$ a solution.

b. Substitute 8 for x.

$$x - 3 = 5$$
$$\boxed{} - 3 \overset{?}{=} 5$$
$$\boxed{}\ \boxed{}\ 5$$

Answer: 8 $\boxed{}$ a solution.

Write the verbal sentence as an equation.

1. The sum of *x* and 7 is 12.
2. The quotient of *n* and 4 is 16.
3. Tell whether 8 or 10 is a solution of $x - 4 = 6$.

Example 3	Solving Equations Using Mental Math		
Equation	**Question**	**Solution**	**Check**
a. $x + 4 = 7$			$\boxed{} + 4 = 7$
b. $12 - n = 5$			$12 - \boxed{} = 5$
c. $18 = 3t$			$18 = 3(\boxed{})$
d. $\dfrac{y}{4} = -5$			$\dfrac{\boxed{}}{4} = -5$

✔ **Checkpoint** Solve the equation using mental math.

4. $x - 8 = 10$	**5.** $24 = 4m$	**6.** $\dfrac{c}{3} = 9$

Solving Equations Using Addition or Subtraction

Goal: Solve equations using addition or subtraction.

Vocabulary

Inverse operations:

Equivalent equations:

Subtraction Property of Equality

Words Subtracting the same number from each side of an equation produces an equivalent equation.

Numbers If $x + 3 = 5$, then $x + 3 - \boxed{} = 5 - \boxed{}$, or $x = \boxed{}$.

Algebra If $x + a = b$, then $x + a - \boxed{} = b - \boxed{}$, or $x = \boxed{}$.

Example 1 Solving an Equation Using Subtraction

Solve $x + 5 = -2$.

Solution

> When you solve an equation, your goal is to write an equivalent equation that has the variable by itself on one side. This process is called *solving for the variable*.

Use the subtraction property of equality to solve for x.

$$x + 5 = -2 \qquad \text{Write original equation.}$$

$$x + 5 - \boxed{} = -2 - \boxed{} \qquad \text{Subtract } \boxed{} \text{ from each side.}$$

$$x = \boxed{} \qquad \text{Simplify.}$$

Answer: The solution is $\boxed{}$.

Check: $\quad x + 5 = -2 \qquad$ Write original equation.

$\qquad \boxed{} + 5 \overset{?}{=} -2 \qquad$ Substitute for x.

$\qquad \boxed{}\boxed{} -2 \qquad \boxed{}$.

Addition Property of Equality

Words Adding the same number to each side of an equation produces an equivalent equation.

Numbers If $x - 3 = 5$, then $x - 3 + \boxed{} = 5 + \boxed{}$, or $x = \boxed{}$.

Algebra If $x - a = b$, then $x - a + \boxed{} = b + \boxed{}$, or $x = \boxed{}$.

Example 2 *Solving an Equation Using Addition*

Solve $12 = y - 7$.

Solution

Use the addition property of equality to solve for y.

$$12 = y - 7 \qquad \text{Write original equation.}$$

$$12 + \boxed{} = y - 7 + \boxed{} \qquad \text{Add } \boxed{} \text{ to each side.}$$

$$\boxed{} = y \qquad \text{Simplify.}$$

Answer: The solution is $\boxed{}$.

✔ *Checkpoint* **Solve the equation. Check your solution.**

1. $x + 6 = 19$	**2.** $-5 = y + 12$	**3.** $m - 3 = -11$

2.6 Solving Equations Using Multiplication or Division

Goal: Solve equations using multiplication or division.

Division Property of Equality

Words Dividing each side of an equation by the same nonzero number produces an equivalent equation.

Numbers If $3x = 12$, then $\dfrac{3x}{\boxed{}} = \dfrac{12}{\boxed{}}$, or $x = \boxed{}$.

Algebra If $ax = b$ and $a \neq 0$, then $\dfrac{ax}{\boxed{}} = \dfrac{b}{\boxed{}}$, or $x = \boxed{}$.

> Remember that you cannot divide a number or an expression by 0.

Example 1 Solving an Equation Using Division

Solve $-7x = 42$.

Solution

$-7x = 42$	Write original equation.
$\dfrac{-7x}{\boxed{}} = \dfrac{42}{\boxed{}}$	Divide each side by $\boxed{}$.
$x = \boxed{}$	Simplify.

Answer: The solution is $\boxed{}$.

Check:

$-7x = 42$	Write original equation.
$-7\left(\boxed{}\right) \stackrel{?}{=} 42$	Substitute for x.
$\boxed{}\ \boxed{}\ 42$	$\boxed{}$.

✔ *Checkpoint* **Solve the equation. Check your solution.**

1. $5x = 45$	**2.** $-56 = -8y$

Multiplication Property of Equality

Words Multiplying each side of an equation by the same nonzero number produces an equivalent equation.

Numbers If $\frac{x}{3} = 12$, then $\boxed{} \cdot \frac{x}{3} = \boxed{} \cdot 12$, or $x = \boxed{}$.

Algebra If $\frac{x}{a} = b$ and $a \neq 0$, then $\boxed{} \cdot \frac{x}{a} = \boxed{} \cdot b$, or $x = \boxed{}$.

Example 2   *Solving an Equation Using Multiplication*

Solve $5 = \frac{w}{11}$.

Solution

$5 = \dfrac{w}{11}$ Write original equation.

$\boxed{} \cdot 5 = \boxed{} \cdot \dfrac{w}{11}$ Multiply each side by $\boxed{}$.

$\boxed{} = w$ Simplify.

Answer: The solution is $\boxed{}$.

 Checkpoint   Solve the equation. Check your solution.

3. $\frac{m}{4} = 11$	4. $-9 = \frac{c}{6}$

2.7 Decimal Operations and Equations with Decimals

Goal: Solve equations involving decimals.

Example 1   *Adding and Subtracting Decimals*

a. Find the sum $-1.7 + (-3.4)$.

Use the rule for adding numbers with the same sign. Add [   ] and [   ]. Both decimals are [   ], so the

sum is [   ].

$$-1.7 + (-3.4) = \boxed{}$$

b. Find the difference $-21.29 - (-34.62)$.

First rewrite the difference as a sum: $-21.29 + 34.62$. Then

use the rule for adding numbers with different signs. Subtract

[   ] from [   ]. [   ] $>$ [   ], so the sum

has the same sign as [ ].

$$-21.29 - (-34.62) = \boxed{}$$

✓ **Checkpoint**   Find the sum or difference.

1. $-2.8 + (-5.9)$	**2.** $7.12 - (-3.46)$

Example 2   Multiplying and Dividing Decimals

a. $-0.4(13.7) = $ ☐   Different signs: Product is ☐ .

b. $-2.5(-6.75) = $ ☐   Same signs: Product is ☐ .

c. $-23.49 \div (-2.9) = $ ☐   Same signs: Quotient is ☐ .

d. $18.05 \div (-1.9) = $ ☐   Different signs: Quotient is ☐ .

✓ **Checkpoint**   Find the product or quotient.

3. $-2.8(-5.9)$	4. $7.093 \div (-3.46)$

Example 3   Solving Addition and Subtraction Equations

Solve the equation.

a. $x + 6.3 = 4.8$ b. $y - 5.74 = -3.51$

Solution

a. $x + 6.3 = 4.8$ Write original equation.

$x + 6.3 - $ ☐ $= 4.8 - $ ☐   Subtract ☐ from each side.

$x = $ ☐   Simplify.

b. $y - 5.74 = -3.51$ Write original equation.

$y - 5.74 + $ ☐ $= -3.51 + $ ☐   Add ☐ to each side.

$y = $ ☐   Simplify.

✓ **Checkpoint** **Solve the equation. Check your solution.**

5. $x + 5.6 = 9.4$	**6.** $-3.5 = y + 1.2$	**7.** $m - 5.3 = -7.2$

Example 4 **Solving Multiplication and Division Equations**

Solve the equation.

a. $0.8m = 4.8$ **b.** $\dfrac{n}{5} = -2.15$

Solution

a. $0.8m = 4.8$ Write original equation.

$\dfrac{0.8m}{\boxed{}} = \dfrac{4.8}{\boxed{}}$ Divide each side by $\boxed{}$.

$m = \boxed{}$ Simplify.

b. $\dfrac{n}{5} = -2.15$ Write original equation.

$\boxed{}\left(\dfrac{n}{5}\right) = \boxed{}(-2.15)$ Multiply each side by $\boxed{}$.

$n = \boxed{}$ Simplify.

✓ **Checkpoint** **Solve the equation. Check your solution.**

8. $6x = -43.2$	**9.** $\dfrac{y}{-3.1} = -8.4$

Words to Review

Give an example of the vocabulary word.

Additive identity	Multiplicative identity

Equivalent numerical expressions	Equivalent variable expressions

Term, coefficient, constant term, like terms	Equation

Solution of an equation	Solving an equation

Inverse operations	Equivalent equations

Review your notes and Chapter 2 by using the Chapter Review on pages 108–111 of your textbook.

3.1 Solving Two-Step Equations

Goal: Solve two-step equations.

Example 1   *Using Subtraction and Division to Solve*

Solve $4x + 9 = -7$. Check your solution.

$4x + 9 = -7$	Write original equation.
$4x + 9 - \boxed{} = -7 - \boxed{}$	Subtract $\boxed{}$ from each side.
$4x = \boxed{}$	Simplify.
$\dfrac{4x}{\boxed{}} = \dfrac{-16}{\boxed{}}$	Divide each side by $\boxed{}$.
$x = \boxed{}$	Simplify.

Answer: The solution is $\boxed{}$.

Check: $4x + 9 = -7$	Write original equation.
$4\left(\boxed{}\right) + 9 \overset{?}{=} -7$	Substitute for x.
$\boxed{}\ \boxed{} -7$	$\boxed{}$.

✔ **Checkpoint**   Solve the equation. Check your solution.

1. $3x + 8 = 26$	**2.** $-21 = 4x + 7$

Example 2 *Using Addition and Multiplication to Solve*

Solve $\frac{x}{3} - 4 = -1$. **Check your solution.**

$\frac{x}{3} - 4 = -1$	Write original equation.
$\frac{x}{3} - 4 + \boxed{} = -1 + \boxed{}$	Add $\boxed{}$ to each side.
$\frac{x}{3} = \boxed{}$	Simplify.
$\boxed{}\left(\frac{x}{3}\right) = \boxed{}\left(\boxed{}\right)$	Multiply each side by $\boxed{}$.
$x = \boxed{}$	Simplify.

Answer: The solution is $\boxed{}$.

Check:

$\frac{x}{3} - 4 = -1$	Write original equation.
$\dfrac{\boxed{}}{3} - 4 \overset{?}{=} -1$	Substitute for x.
$\boxed{}\ \boxed{}\ -1$	$\boxed{}$.

✔ *Checkpoint* **Solve the equation. Check your solution.**

3. $\frac{x}{4} - 7 = 2$	4. $8 = \frac{b}{5} - 3$

Example 3 **Solving an Equation with Negative Coefficients**

Solve $2 - 3x = 17$. Check your solution.

$2 - 3x = 17$	Write original equation.
$2 - 3x - \boxed{} = 17 - \boxed{}$	Subtract $\boxed{}$ from each side.
$-3x = \boxed{}$	Simplify.
$\dfrac{-3x}{\boxed{}} = \dfrac{15}{\boxed{}}$	Divide each side by $\boxed{}$.
$x = \boxed{}$	Simplify.

Answer: The solution is $\boxed{}$.

Check:

$2 - 3x = 17$	Write original equation.
$2 - 3\left(\boxed{}\right) \stackrel{?}{=} 17$	Substitute for x.
$\boxed{}\ \boxed{}\ 17$	$\boxed{}$.

✔ *Checkpoint* **Solve the equation. Check your solution.**

5. $3 - 2y = 19$	**6.** $-5 = 4 - m$

3.2 Solving Equations Having Like Terms and Parentheses

Goal: Solve equations using the distributive property.

Example 1   *Writing and Solving an Equation*

Baseball Game A group of five friends are going to a baseball game. Tickets for the game cost $12 each, or $60 for the group. The group also wants to eat at the game. Hot dogs cost $2.75 each and bottled water costs $1.25 each. The group has a total budget of $76. If the group buys the same number of hot dogs and bottles of water, how many can they afford to buy?

Solution

Let *n* represent the number of hot dogs and the number of bottles of water. Then 2.75*n* represents the cost of *n* hot dogs and 1.25*n* represents the cost of *n* bottles of water. Write a verbal model.

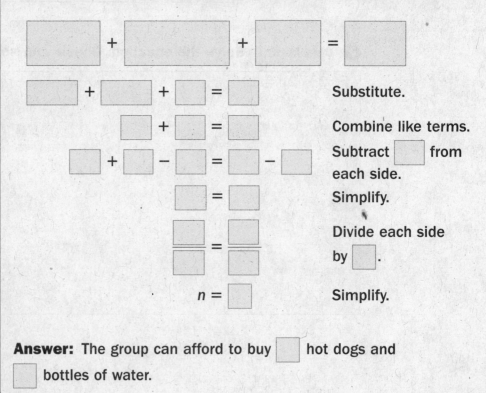

$$\boxed{} + \boxed{} + \boxed{} = \boxed{}$$

$$\boxed{} + \boxed{} + \boxed{} = \boxed{} \qquad \text{Substitute.}$$

$$\boxed{} + \boxed{} = \boxed{} \qquad \text{Combine like terms.}$$

$$\boxed{} + \boxed{} - \boxed{} = \boxed{} - \boxed{} \qquad \text{Subtract } \boxed{} \text{ from each side.}$$

$$\boxed{} = \boxed{} \qquad \text{Simplify.}$$

$$\frac{\boxed{}}{\boxed{}} = \frac{\boxed{}}{\boxed{}} \qquad \text{Divide each side by } \boxed{}.$$

$$n = \boxed{} \qquad \text{Simplify.}$$

Answer: The group can afford to buy $\boxed{}$ hot dogs and $\boxed{}$ bottles of water.

Example 2 **Solving Equations Using the Distributive Property**

Solve the equation.

a. $-24 = 6(2 - x)$ **b.** $-2(7 - 4x) = 10$

Solution

a.

$-24 = 6(2 - x)$		Write original equation.
$-24 = \boxed{}$		Distributive property
$-24 - \boxed{} = \boxed{} - \boxed{}$		Subtract $\boxed{}$ from each side.
$\boxed{} = \boxed{}$		Simplify.
$\dfrac{\boxed{}}{\boxed{}} = \dfrac{\boxed{}}{\boxed{}}$		Divide each side by $\boxed{}$.
$\boxed{} = x$		Simplify.

b.

$-2(7 - 4x) = 10$		Write original equation.
$\boxed{} = 10$		Distributive property
$\boxed{} + \boxed{} = 10 + \boxed{}$		Add $\boxed{}$ to each side.
$\boxed{} = \boxed{}$		Simplify.
$\dfrac{\boxed{}}{\boxed{}} = \dfrac{\boxed{}}{\boxed{}}$		Divide each side by $\boxed{}$.
$x = \boxed{}$		Simplify.

Example 3 **Combining Like Terms After Distributing**

Solve $6x - 4(x - 1) = 14$.

$6x - 4(x - 1) = 14$ Write original equation.

$6x$ $= 14$ Distributive property

$\boxed{} = 14$ Combine like terms.

$\boxed{} - \boxed{} = 14 - \boxed{}$ Subtract $\boxed{}$ from each side.

$\boxed{} = \boxed{}$ Simplify.

$\dfrac{\boxed{}}{\boxed{}} = \dfrac{\boxed{}}{\boxed{}}$ Divide each side by $\boxed{}$.

$x = \boxed{}$ Simplify.

✓ *Checkpoint* **Solve the equation. Check your solution.**

1. $-20 = 5(3 - x)$	**2.** $4y - 14 + 3y = 28$
3. $-3(6 - 2x) = 12$	**4.** $5x - 2(x - 3) = 30$

3.3 Solving Equations with Variables on Both Sides

Goal: Solve equations with variables on both sides.

Solve $5n - 7 = 9n + 21$.

$5n - 7 = 9n + 21$	Write original equation.
$5n - 7 - \boxed{} = 9n + 21 - \boxed{}$	Subtract $\boxed{}$ from each side.
$-7 = \boxed{} + 21$	Simplify.
$-7 - \boxed{} = \boxed{} + 21 - \boxed{}$	Subtract $\boxed{}$ from each side.
$\boxed{} = \boxed{}$	Simplify.
$\dfrac{\boxed{}}{\boxed{}} = \dfrac{\boxed{}}{\boxed{}}$	Divide each side by $\boxed{}$.
$\boxed{} = n$	Simplify.

Answer: The solution is $\boxed{}$.

Example 2 *An Equation with No Solution*

Solve $3(2x + 1) = 6x$.

$3(2x + 1) = 6x$	Write original equation.
$\boxed{} = 6x$	Distributive property

Notice that this statement $\boxed{}$ true because the number $6x$ $\boxed{}$. The equation has $\boxed{}$ $\boxed{}$. As a check, you can continue solving the equation.

$\boxed{} = 6x \boxed{}$	Subtract $\boxed{}$ from each side.
$\boxed{} = \boxed{}$	Simplify.

The statement $\boxed{}$ $\boxed{}$ true, so the equation has $\boxed{}$.

Example 3 **Solving an Equation with All Numbers as Solutions**

Solve $4(x + 2) = 4x + 8$.

$$4(x + 2) = 4x + 8 \qquad \text{Write original equation.}$$

$$\boxed{} = 4x + 8 \qquad \text{Distributive property}$$

Notice that for all values of x, the statement $\boxed{} = 4x + 8$ is $\boxed{}$. The equation has $\boxed{}$.

✔ *Checkpoint* **Solve the equation. Check your solution.**

1. $3n - 6 = 5n + 20$	**2.** $12x = 4(3x - 1)$
3. $3(2n + 4) = 2(3n + 6)$	**4.** $2x + 7 = -2x - 13$

Example 4   *Solving an Equation to Find a Perimeter*

Geometry Find the perimeter of the square.

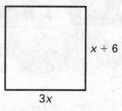

$x + 6$

$3x$

Solution

1. A square has four sides of equal length. Write an equation and solve for x.

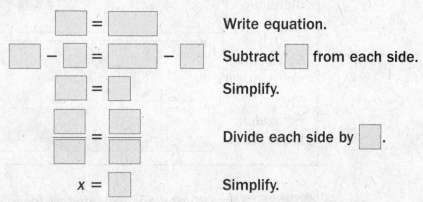

$\boxed{} = \boxed{}$ Write equation.

$\boxed{} - \boxed{} = \boxed{} - \boxed{}$ Subtract $\boxed{}$ from each side.

$\boxed{} = \boxed{}$ Simplify.

$\dfrac{\boxed{}}{\boxed{}} = \dfrac{\boxed{}}{\boxed{}}$ Divide each side by $\boxed{}$.

$x = \boxed{}$ Simplify.

2. Find the length of one side by substituting $\boxed{}$ for x in either expression.

$3x = 3\left(\boxed{}\right) = \boxed{}$ Substitute for x and multiply.

3. To find the perimeter, multiply the length of one side by $\boxed{}$.

$\boxed{} \cdot \boxed{} = \boxed{}$

Answer: The perimeter of the square is $\boxed{}$ units.

✓ *Checkpoint*   **Find the perimeter of the square.**

5.

$3x + 8$

$5x$

Solving Inequalities Using Addition or Subtraction

Goal: Solve inequalities using addition or subtraction.

Vocabulary

Inequality:

Solution of an inequality:

Equivalent inequalities:

Example 1 *Writing and Graphing an Inequality*

Air Travel An airline allows passengers to carry on-board one piece of luggage. Luggage that exceeds 40 pounds cannot be carried on-board. Write an inequality that gives the weight of luggage that cannot be carried on-board.

Solution

Let w represent the weight of the luggage. Because the weight cannot exceed 40 pounds, the weight of luggage that cannot be carried on-board must be   .

Answer: The inequality is   . Draw the graph below.

```
<----+---+---+---+---+---+---+---+---+---->
     0  10  20  30  40  50  60  70  80
```

Addition and Subtraction Properties of Inequality

Words Adding or subtracting the same number on each side of an inequality produces an equivalent inequality.

Algebra If $a < b$, then $a + c < b + c$ and $a - c < b - c$.

If $a > b$, then $a + c > b + c$ and $a - c > b - c$.

The addition and subtraction properties of inequality are also true for inequalities involving $\leq$ and $\geq$.

Example 2 *Solving an Inequality Using Subtraction*

Solve $m + 9 \leq 12$. Graph and check your solution.

$m + 9 \leq 12$ Write original inequality.

$m + 9 - \boxed{} \leq 12 - \boxed{}$ Subtract $\boxed{}$ from each side.

$m \leq \boxed{}$ Simplify.

Answer: The solution is $m \leq \boxed{}$. Draw the graph below.

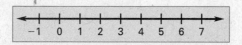

Check: Choose any number less than or equal to $\boxed{}$. Substitute the number into the original inequality.

$m + 9 \leq 12$ Write original inequality.

$\boxed{} + 9 \overset{?}{\leq} 12$ Substitute 0 for m.

$\boxed{}\ \boxed{}\ 12$ $\boxed{}$.

Example 3 *Solving an Inequality Using Addition*

Solve $-7 < x - 11$. Graph your solution.

$-7 < x - 11$ Write original inequality.

$-7 + \boxed{} < x - 11 + \boxed{}$ Add $\boxed{}$ to each side.

$\boxed{} < x$ Simplify.

Answer: The solution is $\boxed{} < x$, or $\boxed{}$. Draw the graph below.

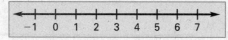

You can read an inequality from left to right as well as from right to left. For instance, "2 is greater than x" can also be read "x is less than 2." Algebraically, this means that $2 > x$ can also be written as $x < 2$.

✓ **Checkpoint** **Solve the inequality. Graph and check your solution.**

1. $m + 7 < 13$

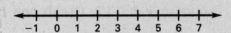

2. $a + 4 \geq 5$

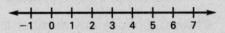

3. $x - 2 \leq 3$

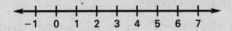

4. $-6 < z - 7$

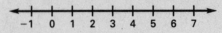

3.5 Solving Inequalities Using Multiplication or Division

Goal: Solve inequalities using multiplication or division.

Multiplication Property of Inequality

Words Multiplying each side of an inequality by a *positive* number produces an equivalent inequality.

Multiplying each side of an inequality by a *negative* number and *reversing the direction of the inequality symbol* produces an equivalent inequality.

> The multiplication properties of inequality are also true for inequalities involving $>$, $\leq$, and $\geq$.

Algebra If $a < b$ and $c > 0$, then ac ☐ bc.

If $a < b$ and $c < 0$, then ac ☐ bc.

Example 1   *Solving an Inequality Using Multiplication*

Solve $\dfrac{m}{-4} > 2$.

$$\frac{m}{-4} > 2 \qquad \text{Write original inequality.}$$

$$\boxed{}\left(\frac{m}{-4}\right) \boxed{} \boxed{} \cdot 2 \qquad \begin{array}{l}\text{Multiply each side by } \boxed{}.\\ \text{Reverse inequality symbol.}\end{array}$$

$$m \; \boxed{} \; \boxed{} \qquad \text{Simplify.}$$

✓ **Checkpoint** Solve the inequality. Graph your solution.

1. $\dfrac{t}{5} < 3$	**2.** $\dfrac{b}{-8} \leq 1$

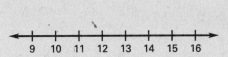

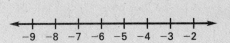

Division Property of Inequality

Words Dividing each side of an inequality by a *positive* number produces an equivalent inequality.

Dividing each side of an inequality by a *negative* number and *reversing the direction of the inequality symbol* produces an equivalent inequality.

Algebra If $a < b$ and $c > 0$, then $\dfrac{a}{c}$ ▢ $\dfrac{b}{c}$.

If $a < b$ and $c < 0$, then $\dfrac{a}{c}$ ▢ $\dfrac{b}{c}$.

> The division properties of inequality are also true for inequalities involving >, ≤, and ≥.

Example 2   Solving an Inequality Using Division

Solve $-11t \geq 33$.

$-11t \geq 33$ Write original inequality.

$\dfrac{-11t}{\boxed{}} \boxed{} \dfrac{33}{\boxed{}}$ Divide each side by ▢. Reverse inequality symbol.

$t \boxed{} \boxed{}$ Simplify.

✔ **Checkpoint** Solve the inequality. Graph your solution.

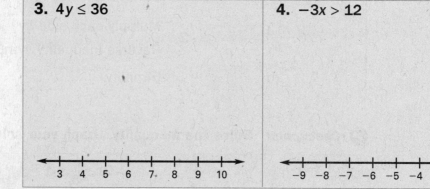

3. $4y \leq 36$

4. $-3x > 12$

3.6 Solving Multi-Step Inequalities

Goal: Solve multi-step inequalities.

Example 1   *Writing and Solving a Multi-Step Inequality*

Charity Walk You are participating in a charity walk. You want to raise at least $500 for the charity. You already have $175 by asking people to pledge $25 each. How many more $25 pledges do you need?

Solution

Let p represent the number of additional pledges. Write a verbal model.

$$\boxed{} \; + \; \boxed{} \; \cdot \; \boxed{} \; \geq \; \boxed{}$$

$$\boxed{} + \boxed{} \geq \boxed{} \qquad \text{Substitute.}$$

$$\boxed{} + \boxed{} - \boxed{} \geq \boxed{} - \boxed{} \qquad \text{Subtract } \boxed{} \text{ from each side.}$$

$$\boxed{} \geq \boxed{} \qquad \text{Simplify.}$$

$$\frac{\boxed{}}{\boxed{}} \geq \frac{\boxed{}}{\boxed{}} \qquad \text{Divide each side by } \boxed{}.$$

$$p \geq \boxed{} \qquad \text{Simplify.}$$

Answer: You need at least $\boxed{}$ more $25 pledges.

✓ **Checkpoint**

1. Look back at Example 1. Suppose you wanted to raise at least $620 and you already have raised $380 by asking people to pledge $20 each. How many more $20 pledges do you need?

Example 2 *Solving a Multi-Step Inequality*

$$\frac{x}{-3} - 9 < -7 \qquad \text{Original inequality}$$

$$\frac{x}{-3} - 9 + \boxed{} < -7 + \boxed{} \qquad \text{Add } \boxed{} \text{ to each side.}$$

$$\frac{x}{-3} < \boxed{} \qquad \text{Simplify.}$$

$$\boxed{}\left(\frac{x}{-3}\right) \boxed{} \; \boxed{} \cdot \boxed{} \qquad \begin{array}{l} \text{Multiply each side by } \boxed{}. \\ \text{Reverse inequality symbol.} \end{array}$$

$$x \; \boxed{} \; \boxed{} \qquad \text{Simplify.}$$

✔ *Checkpoint* **Solve the inequality. Then graph the solution.**

2. $2x + 9 < 25$	**3.** $-3 \geq \dfrac{x}{-4} - 2$

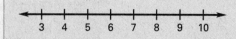

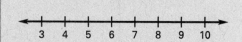

4. $2 \geq -4 - x$	**5.** $\dfrac{x}{2} + 4 \leq 9$

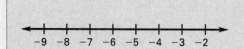

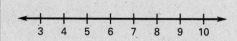

3

Words to Review

Give an example of the vocabulary word.

Inequality

Solution of an inequality

Equivalent inequalities

Review your notes and Chapter 3 by using the Chapter Review on pages 154–157 of your textbook.

Factors and Prime Factorization

Goal: Write the prime factorization of a number.

Vocabulary

Prime number:

Composite number:

Prime factorization:

Factor tree:

Monomial:

Example 1 | **Writing Factors**

A rectangle has an area of 18 square feet. Find all possible whole number dimensions of the rectangle.

1. Write 18 as a product of two whole numbers in all possible ways.

☐ · ☐ = 18   ☐ · ☐ = 18   ☐ · ☐ = 18

The factors of 18 are _____ .

2. Use the factors to find all rectangles with an area of 18 square feet that have whole number dimensions. Then label the given rectangles.

> The area of a rectangle can be found using the formula, Area = length × width.
>
> ☐ width
> length

Example 2   *Writing a Prime Factorization*

Write the prime factorization of 420.

One possible factor tree:

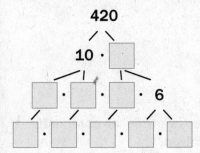

Write original number.

Write 420 as 10 · ☐.

Write 10 as ☐ · ☐. Write ☐ as

☐ · 6.

Write 6 as ☐ · ☐.

Another possible factor tree:

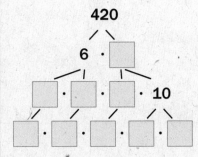

Write original number.

Write 420 as 6 · ☐.

Write 6 as ☐ · ☐. Write ☐ as

☐ · 10.

Write 10 as ☐ · ☐.

Both trees give the same result: 420 = [   ].

Answer: The prime factorization of 420 is [   ].

Example 3   *Factoring a Monomial*

Factor the monomial $24x^4y$.

$24x^4y =$ [   ] $\cdot x^4y$ Write 24 as [   ].

    $=$ [   ] $\cdot y$ Write x^4 as [   ].

1. 28	**2.** 48

Tell whether the number is *prime* or *composite*. If it is composite, write its prime factorization.

3. 97	**4.** 117

Factor the monomial.

5. $21n^5$	**6.** $18x^2y^3$

4.2 Greatest Common Factor

Goal: Find the greatest common factor of two or more numbers.

Vocabulary

Common factor:

Greatest common factor (GCF):

Relatively prime:

Example 1   *Finding the Greatest Common Factor*

Volunteers A high school asks for volunteers to help clean up local highways on one Saturday each month. The group of volunteers has 27 freshman, 18 sophomores, 36 juniors, and 45 seniors. What is the greatest number of groups that can be formed if each group is to have the same number of each type of student? How many freshman, sophomores, juniors, and seniors will be in each group?

Solution

Method 1 List the factors of each number. Identify the greatest number that is on every list.

Factors of 27:

Factors of 18:

Factors of 36:

Factors of 45:

The common factors are

.

The GCF is

.

Method 2 Write the prime factorization of each number. The GCF is the product of the prime factors.

$27 =$ ⬚

$18 =$ ⬚

$36 =$ ⬚

$45 =$ ⬚

The common prime factors are ⬚.

The GCF is ⬚.

Answer: The greatest number of groups that can be formed is ⬚.

Each group will have $27 \div$ ⬚ $=$ ⬚ freshman, $18 \div$ ⬚ $=$ ⬚ sophomores, $36 \div$ ⬚ $=$ ⬚ juniors, and $45 \div$ ⬚ $=$ ⬚ seniors.

✓ **Checkpoint** Find the greatest common factor of the numbers.

1. 54, 81	**2.** 12, 48, 66

Example 2 *Identifying Relatively Prime Numbers*

Find the greatest common factor of the numbers. Then tell whether the numbers are relatively prime.

a. 28, 63   **b.** 42, 55

Solution

a. List the factors of each number. Identify the greatest number that the lists have in common.

Factors of 28: ⬚

Factors of 63: ⬚

The GCF is ⬚. So, the numbers ⬚ relatively prime.

b. Write the prime factorization of each number.

$42 =$ ⬚ $55 =$ ⬚

The GCF is ⬚. So, the numbers ⬚ relatively prime.

✓ Checkpoint Find the greatest common factor of the numbers. Then tell whether the numbers are relatively prime.

3. 30, 49	**4.** 52, 78

Example 3 *Finding the GCF of Monomials*

Find the greatest common factor of $16x^2y$ and $26x^2y^3$.

Solution

Factor the monomials. The GCF is the product of the common factors.

$16x^2y = $ [_____]

$26x^2y^3 = $ [_____]

Answer: The GCF is [____].

✓ Checkpoint Find the greatest common factor of the monomials.

5. $12x^3$, $18x^2$	**6.** $40xy^3$, $24xy$

4.3 Equivalent Fractions

Goal: Write equivalent fractions.

Vocabulary

Equivalent fractions:

Simplest form:

Equivalent Fractions

Words To write equivalent fractions, multiply or divide the numerator and the denominator by the same nonzero number.

Algebra For all numbers a, b, and c, where $b \neq 0$ and $c \neq 0$,

$$\frac{a}{b} = \frac{a \cdot c}{b \cdot c} \text{ and } \frac{a}{b} = \frac{a \div c}{b \div c}.$$

Numbers $\frac{1}{3} = \frac{1 \cdot 2}{3 \cdot 2} = \frac{2}{6}$ $\qquad$ $\frac{2}{6} = \frac{2 \div 2}{6 \div 2} = \frac{1}{3}$

Example 1 *Writing Equivalent Fractions*

Write two fractions that are equivalent to $\frac{6}{18}$.

Multiply or divide the numerator and the denominator by the

$\frac{6}{18} = \frac{6 \cdot 2}{18 \cdot 2} = \boxed{}$ $\qquad$ Multiply numerator and denominator by 2.

$\frac{6}{18} = \frac{6 \div 3}{18 \div 3} = \boxed{}$ $\qquad$ Divide numerator and denominator by 3.

Answer: The fractions $\boxed{}$ and $\boxed{}$ are equivalent to $\frac{6}{18}$.

✔ Checkpoint Write two fractions that are equivalent to the given fraction.

1. $\frac{7}{14}$	2. $\frac{4}{16}$	3. $\frac{10}{25}$

Example 2 *Writing a Fraction in Simplest Form*

Write $\frac{8}{36}$ in simplest form.

Write the prime factorizations of the numerator and denominator.

$8 = $ ☐ $36 = $ ☐

The GCF of 8 and 36 is ☐.

$\frac{8}{36} = \frac{8 \div \boxed{}}{36 \div \boxed{}}$ Divide numerator and denominator by GCF.

$= \boxed{}$ Simplify.

✔ Checkpoint Write the fraction in simplest form.

4. $\frac{3}{18}$	5. $\frac{12}{32}$	6. $\frac{24}{42}$

Example 3 *Simplifying a Variable Expression*

Write $\dfrac{14x^2y}{35x^3}$ in simplest form.

$\dfrac{14x^2y}{35x^3} = \dfrac{\boxed{}}{\boxed{}}$ Factor numerator and denominator.

$= \dfrac{\boxed{}\ \boxed{}\ \boxed{}}{\boxed{}}$

$\dfrac{\boxed{}}{\boxed{}\ \boxed{}\ \boxed{}}$ Divide out common factors.

$= \boxed{}$ Simplify.

✔ **Checkpoint** Write the variable expression in simplest form.

7. $\dfrac{9a}{15a^2}$	8. $\dfrac{16mn^2}{28n}$	9. $\dfrac{39st^2}{3s^2t}$

4.4 Least Common Multiple

Goal: Find the least common multiple of two numbers.

Vocabulary

Multiple:

Common multiple:

Least common multiple (LCM):

Least common denominator (LCD):

Example 1 *Finding the Least Common Multiple*

Find the least common multiple of 6 and 14.

Solution

You can use one of two methods to find the LCM.

Method 1 List the multiples of each number. Identify the least number that is on both lists.

Multiples of 6:

Multiples of 14:

The LCM of 6 and 14 is ☐.

Method 2 Find the common factors of the numbers.

6 = ☐

14 = ☐

The common factor is ☐.

Multiply all of the factors, using each common factor only once.

LCM = ☐ = ☐

Answer: Both methods get the same result. The LCM is ☐.

Example 2   *Finding the Least Common Multiple of Monomials*

Find the least common multiple 6xy and $16x^2$.

$6xy =$ [ ]

$16x^2 =$ [ ]

LCM = [ ]   = [ ]

Answer: The least common multiple of 6xy and $16x^2$ is [ ].

✓ *Checkpoint*   **Find the least common multiple of the numbers or the monomials.**

1. 8, 18	**2.** 4, 5, 15
3. 12x, $18x^2$	**4.** 4xy, $10xz^2$

Example 3   *Comparing Fractions Using the LCD*

Summer Sports Last year, a summer resort had 165,000 visitors, including 44,000 water skiers. This year, the resort had 180,000 visitors, including 63,000 water skiers. In which year was the fraction of water skiers greater?

Solution

1. Write the fractions and simplify.

Last year: $\dfrac{\text{Number of water skiers}}{\text{Total number of visitors}}$ = [ ] = [ ]

This year: $\dfrac{\text{Number of water skiers}}{\text{Total number of visitors}}$ = [ ] = [ ]

2. Find the LCD of [ ] and [ ]. The LCM of [ ] and [ ] is

[ ]. So, the LCD of the fractions is [ ].

3. Write equivalent fractions using the LCD.

Last year: ▢ = ▢ = ▢

This year: ▢ = ▢ = ▢

4. Compare the numerators: ▢ < ▢ , so ▢ < ▢ .

Answer: The fraction of water skiers was greater ▢ .

Example 4   *Ordering Fractions and Mixed Numbers*

Order the numbers $4\frac{5}{12}$, $\frac{9}{2}$, and $\frac{33}{8}$ from least to greatest.

1. Write the mixed number as an improper fraction.

$$4\frac{5}{12} = \frac{\boxed{}}{12} = \frac{\boxed{}}{12}$$

2. Find the LCD of $\frac{\boxed{}}{12}$, $\frac{9}{2}$, and $\frac{33}{8}$. The LCM of 12, 2, and 8 is ▢ . So, the LCD is ▢ .

3. Write equivalent fractions using the LCD.

$$\frac{\boxed{}}{12} = \frac{\boxed{} \cdot \boxed{}}{12 \cdot \boxed{}} = \boxed{} \qquad \frac{9}{2} = \frac{9 \cdot \boxed{}}{2 \cdot \boxed{}} = \boxed{}$$

$$\frac{33}{8} = \frac{33 \cdot \boxed{}}{8 \cdot \boxed{}} = \boxed{}$$

4. Compare the numerators: ▢ < ▢ and ▢ < ▢ ,

so ▢ < ▢ and ▢ < ▢ .

Answer: From least to greatest, the numbers are

▢ , ▢ , and ▢ .

Rules of Exponents

Goal: Multiply and divide powers.

Product of Powers Property

Words To multiply powers with the same base, add their exponents.

Algebra $a^m \cdot a^n = a^{m+n}$

Numbers $4^3 \cdot 4^2 = 4^{\boxed{}} = 4^{\boxed{}}$

Example 1   *Using the Product of Powers Property*

a. $4^7 \cdot 4^{11} = 4^{\boxed{}}$ Product of powers property

$= 4^{\boxed{}}$ Add exponents.

b. $2x^2 \cdot 7x^6 = 2 \cdot 7 \cdot x^2 \cdot x^6$ Commutative property of multiplication

$= 2 \cdot 7 \cdot x^{\boxed{}}$ Product of powers property

$= 2 \cdot 7 \cdot x^{\boxed{}}$ Add exponents.

$= \boxed{}$ Multiply.

✓ **Checkpoint**   **Find the product. Write your answer using exponents.**

1. $2^5 \cdot 2^{12}$	**2.** $5^6 \cdot 5^2 \cdot 5^3$
3. $x^6 \cdot x^{13}$	**4.** $b^2 \cdot b^4 \cdot b$

Quotient of Powers Property

Words To divide powers with the same base, subtract the exponent of the denominator from the exponent of the numerator.

Algebra $\dfrac{a^m}{a^n} = a^{m-n}$, where $a \neq 0$

Numbers $\dfrac{5^7}{5^4} = 5^{\boxed{}} = 5^{\boxed{}}$

Example 2   *Using the Quotient of Powers Property*

a. $\dfrac{6^8}{6^3} = 6^{\boxed{}}$ Quotient of powers property

$= 6^{\boxed{}}$ Subtract exponents.

b. $\dfrac{3x^7}{12x^3} = \dfrac{3x^{\boxed{}}}{12}$ Quotient of powers property

$= \dfrac{3x^{\boxed{}}}{12}$ Subtract exponents.

$= \boxed{}$ Divide numerator and denominator by $\boxed{}$.

✔ **Checkpoint** Find the quotient. Write your answer using exponents.

5. $\dfrac{5^9}{5^2}$	**6.** $\dfrac{12^7}{12^4}$
7. $\dfrac{4x^{13}}{24x^9}$	**8.** $\dfrac{14x^{16}}{6x^{11}}$

Example 3 **Using Both Properties of Powers**

Simplify $\dfrac{4m^3 \cdot m^4}{12m^2}$.

$\dfrac{4m^3 \cdot m^4}{12m^2} = \dfrac{4m^{\boxed{}}}{12m^2}$ Product of powers property

$= \dfrac{4m^{\boxed{}}}{12m^2}$ Add exponents.

$= \dfrac{4m^{\boxed{}}}{12}$ Quotient of powers property

$= \dfrac{4m^{\boxed{}}}{12}$ Subtract exponents.

$= \boxed{}$ Divide numerator and denominator by $\boxed{}$.

✓ *Checkpoint* **Simplify.**

9. $\dfrac{6m^5 \cdot m}{15m^3}$	10. $\dfrac{n^2 \cdot 10n^6}{5n^3}$

4.6 Negative and Zero Exponents

Goal: Work with negative and zero exponents.

Negative and Zero Exponents

For any nonzero number a, $a^0 = 1$.

For any nonzero number a and any integer n, $a^{-n} = \dfrac{1}{a^n}$.

Example 1 *Powers with Negative and Zero Exponents*

Write the expression using only positive exponents.

a. $4^{-3} = $ ☐   Definition of negative exponent

b. $m^{-5}n^0 = m^{-5} \cdot$ ☐   Definition of zero exponent

   $= $ ☐   Definition of negative exponent

c. $13xy^{-8} = $ ☐   Definition of negative exponent

✓ **Checkpoint**   Write the expression using only positive exponents.

1. $33{,}333^0$	2. 7^{-3}	3. $2z^{-2}$	4. $3x^{-4}y$

Example 2 *Rewriting Fractions*

Write the expression without using a fraction bar.

a. $\dfrac{1}{15} = $ ☐   Definition of negative exponent

b. $\dfrac{a^3}{c^5} = $ ☐   Definition of negative exponent

✔ Checkpoint Write the expression without using a fraction bar.

5. $\dfrac{1}{18}$	6. $\dfrac{1}{100}$	7. $\dfrac{3}{c^2}$	8. $\dfrac{x^5}{y^7}$

Example 3 **Using Powers Properties with Negative Exponents**

Find the product or quotient. Write your answer using only positive exponents.

a. $6^{12} \cdot 6^{-4}$

b. $\dfrac{7n^{-4}}{n}$

Solution

a. $6^{12} \cdot 6^{-4} = 6^{\boxed{}}$ Product of powers property

   $= 6^{\boxed{}}$ Add exponents.

b. $\dfrac{7n^{-4}}{n} = 7n^{\boxed{}}$ Quotient of powers property

   $= 7n^{\boxed{}}$ Subtract exponents.

   $= \boxed{}$ Definition of negative exponent

✔ Checkpoint Find the product or quotient. Write your answer using only positive exponents.

9. $3^{10} \cdot 3^{-7}$	10. $\dfrac{7d^{-4}}{d^2}$

4.7 Scientific Notation

Goal: Write numbers using scientific notation.

Using Scientific Notation

A number is written in **scientific notation** if it has the form $c \times 10^n$ where $1 \leq c < 10$ and n is an integer.

Standard form	Product form	Scientific notation
725,000	$7.25 \times 100,000$	7.25×10^5
0.006	6×0.001	6×10^{-3}

Example 1   *Writing Numbers in Scientific Notation*

a. The average distance Mars is from the sun is 141,600,000 miles. Write this number in scientific notation.

Standard form	Product form	Scientific notation

b. The diameter of a quarter-ounce gold American Eagle coin is 0.022 meter. Write this number in scientific notation.

Standard form	Product form	Scientific notation

Example 2   *Writing Numbers in Standard Form*

a. Write 4.1×10^4 in standard form.

Scientific notation	Product form	Standard form

b. Write 7.23×10^{-6} in standard form.

Scientific notation	Product form	Standard form

✔ Checkpoint Write the number in scientific notation.

1. 3,050,000,000	**2.** 0.000082

Write the number in standard form.

3. 6.53×10^7	**4.** 9.2×10^{-4}

Example 3   *Ordering Numbers Using Scientific Notation*

Order 5.3×10^5, 520,000, and 7.5×10^4 from least to greatest.

1. Write each number in scientific notation if necessary.

520,000 = ☐

2. Order the numbers with different powers of 10.

Because $10^{\square} < 10^{\square}$, ☐ < ☐ and

☐ < ☐ .

3. Order the numbers with the same power of 10.

Because ☐ < ☐ , ☐ < ☐ .

4. Write the original numbers in order from least to greatest.

☐ ; ☐ ; ☐

✔ Checkpoint Order the numbers from least to greatest.

5. 23,000; 3.4×10^3; 2.2×10^4

6. 4.5×10^{-4}; 0.000047; 4.8×10^{-5}

Example 4 **Multiplying Numbers in Scientific Notation**

Oxygen Atoms The volume of one mole of oxygen atoms is about 1.736×10^{-5} cubic meters. Find the volume of 1.5×10^{4} moles of oxygen atoms.

Solution

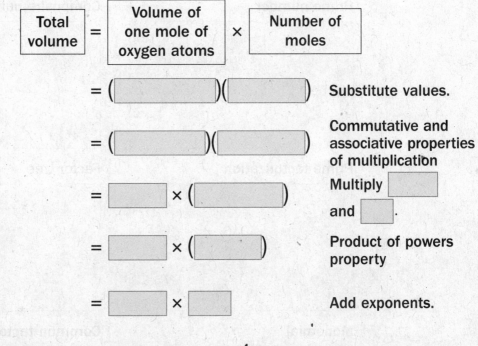

$$\text{Total volume} = \boxed{\text{Volume of one mole of oxygen atoms}} \times \boxed{\text{Number of moles}}$$

$$= (\boxed{})(\boxed{}) \qquad \text{Substitute values.}$$

$$= (\boxed{})(\boxed{}) \qquad \begin{array}{l}\text{Commutative and}\\ \text{associative properties}\\ \text{of multiplication}\end{array}$$

$$= \boxed{} \times (\boxed{}) \qquad \begin{array}{l}\text{Multiply } \boxed{}\\ \text{and } \boxed{}.\end{array}$$

$$= \boxed{} \times (\boxed{}) \qquad \begin{array}{l}\text{Product of powers}\\ \text{property}\end{array}$$

$$= \boxed{} \times \boxed{} \qquad \text{Add exponents.}$$

Answer: The volume of 1.5×10^{4} moles of oxygen atoms is about $\boxed{} \times \boxed{}$ cubic meters.

✔ *Checkpoint* Find the product. Write your answer in scientific notation.

7. $(2.5 \times 10^{3})(2 \times 10^{5})$	8. $(1.5 \times 10^{-2})(4 \times 10^{-4})$

4

Words to Review

Give an example of the vocabulary word.

Prime number

Composite number

Prime factorization

Factor tree

Monomial

Common factor

Greatest common factor (GCF)

Relatively prime

Equivalent fractions

Simplest form

Multiple

Common multiple

Least common multiple (LCM)

Least common denominator (LCD)

Scientific notation

Review your notes and Chapter 4 by using the Chapter Review on pages 210–213 of your textbook.

Goal: Write fractions as decimals and vice versa.

Vocabulary

Rational number:

Terminating decimal:

Repeating decimal:

Example 1   *Identifying Rational Numbers*

Show that the number is rational by writing it as a quotient of two integers.

a. 3   b. -12 c. $4\frac{2}{3}$ d. $-2\frac{1}{4}$

Solution

a. Write the integer 3 as [ ].

b. Write the integer -12 as [ ] or [ ]. These fractions are [ ].

c. Write the mixed number $4\frac{2}{3}$ as the improper fraction [ ].

d. Think of $-2\frac{1}{4}$ as the opposite of [ ]. First write [ ] as [ ].

Then you can write $-2\frac{1}{4}$ as [ ]. To write [ ] as a quotient of two integers, you can assign the negative sign to either the [ ] or the [ ]. You can write [ ] or [ ].

Example 2   *Writing Fractions as Decimals*

a. Write $\frac{5}{16}$ as a decimal.

b. Write $\frac{4}{9}$ as a decimal.

a.
$$
\begin{array}{r}
0.3125 \\
16\overline{)5.0000} \\
4\,8 \\
\overline{20} \\
16 \\
\overline{40} \\
32 \\
\overline{80} \\
80 \\
\overline{0}
\end{array}
$$

Answer: The remainder is [ ], so the decimal is a [＿＿＿＿] decimal:

$\frac{5}{16} = 0.3125.$

b.
$$
\begin{array}{r}
0.44\ldots \\
9\overline{)4.00} \\
3\,6 \\
\overline{40} \\
36
\end{array}
$$

Answer: Use a bar to show the [＿＿＿] in the [＿＿＿] decimal:

$\frac{4}{9} = 0.\overline{4}.$

✔ *Checkpoint*   **Write the fraction or mixed number as a decimal.**

1. $\frac{7}{20}$	**2.** $-\frac{3}{5}$
3. $2\frac{12}{25}$	**4.** $\frac{23}{40}$

Example 3   *Using Decimals to Compare Fractions*

Compare $\frac{42}{48}$ and $\frac{27}{30}$.

$\frac{42}{48} = $ [＿＿＿] and $\frac{27}{30} = $ [＿＿＿]   Divide.

Answer: Compare the decimals. [＿＿＿] > [＿＿＿],

so $\frac{27}{30}$ [＿] $\frac{42}{48}$.

Example 4 **Writing Terminating Decimals as Fractions**

a. $0.03 = \boxed{}$ 3 is in $\boxed{}$ place,

so denominator is $\boxed{}$.

b. $-9.4 = \boxed{}$ 4 is in $\boxed{}$ place,

so denominator is $\boxed{}$.

$= \boxed{}$ Simplify fraction.

Example 5 **Writing a Repeating Decimal as a Fraction**

To write $0.\overline{81}$ as a fraction, let $x = 0.\overline{81}$.

1. Because $0.\overline{81}$ has 2 repeating digits, multiply each side of

$x = 0.\overline{81}$ by $\boxed{}$, or $\boxed{}$. Then $\boxed{}x = \boxed{}$.

$\boxed{}x = \boxed{}$

2. Subtract x from $\boxed{}x$. $-\quad (x = 0.\overline{81})$

$\boxed{}x = \boxed{}$

3. Solve for x and simplify. $\dfrac{\boxed{}x}{\boxed{}} = \dfrac{\boxed{}}{\boxed{}}$

$x = \boxed{}$

Answer: The decimal $0.\overline{81}$ is equivalent to the fraction $\boxed{}$.

5. 0.8

6. −3.75

7. 0.$\overline{12}$

8. 5.$\overline{3}$

Example 6   *Ordering Rational Numbers*

Order the numbers $-\dfrac{17}{2}$, **−1.35, 5.67, −6,** $\dfrac{11}{3}$, $-\dfrac{13}{4}$ **from least to greatest.**

Graph the numbers on the number line. You may want to write improper fractions as mixed numbers.

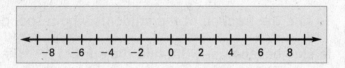

Answer: Read the numbers graphed on the number line from

left to right: ☐ , ☐ , ☐ , ☐ , ☐ , ☐ .

5.2 Adding and Subtracting Like Fractions

Goal: Add and subtract like fractions.

Adding and Subtracting Like Fractions

Words To add or subtract fractions with the same denominator, write the sum or difference of the numerators over the denominator.

Numbers $\dfrac{4}{9} + \dfrac{1}{9} = \dfrac{\boxed{}}{9}$ $\qquad$ $\dfrac{9}{11} - \dfrac{2}{11} = \dfrac{\boxed{}}{11}$

Algebra $\dfrac{a}{c} + \dfrac{b}{c} = \dfrac{\boxed{}}{c}, c \neq 0$ $\qquad$ $\dfrac{a}{c} - \dfrac{b}{c} = \dfrac{\boxed{}}{c}, c \neq 0$

Example 1   Adding Like Fractions

A survey asked 100 students ages 7 to 11 what sports apparel they prefer to wear. The circle graph at the right summarizes their responses. What fraction of the students responded either major league baseball or NBA?

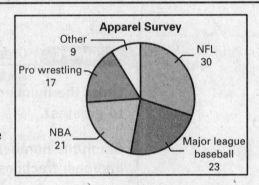

Apparel Survey

- Other 9
- Pro wrestling 17
- NBA 21
- NFL 30
- Major league baseball 23

Solution

To find the fraction of the students who responded either major league baseball or NBA, find the sum of $\boxed{}$ and $\boxed{}$.

$$\boxed{} + \boxed{} = \boxed{}$$ Write sum of numerators over denominator.

$$= \boxed{} = \boxed{}$$ Add. Then simplify.

Answer: The fraction of the students who prefer either major league baseball or NBA apparel is 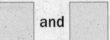 .

Example 2   *Subtracting Like Fractions*

When you perform operations with negative fractions, be sure to assign a negative sign in front of a fraction to the numerator of the fraction.

a. $-\dfrac{4}{9} - \dfrac{3}{9} = \boxed{}$ Write difference of numerators over denominator.

$= \boxed{}$ Subtract.

b. $\dfrac{2}{11} - \left(-\dfrac{4}{11}\right) = \boxed{} + \boxed{}$ To subtract $-\dfrac{4}{11}$, add $\boxed{}$.

$= \boxed{}$ Write sum of numerators over denominator.

$= \boxed{}$ Add.

✓ **Checkpoint**   Find the sum or difference.

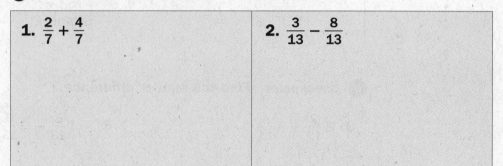

1. $\dfrac{2}{7} + \dfrac{4}{7}$

2. $\dfrac{3}{13} - \dfrac{8}{13}$

Example 3   *Adding and Subtracting Mixed Numbers*

a. $4\dfrac{3}{7} + 3\dfrac{6}{7} = \boxed{} + \boxed{}$ Write mixed numbers as improper fractions.

$= \boxed{}$ Write sum of numerators over denominator.

$= \boxed{} = \boxed{}$ Add. Then write fraction as mixed number.

b. $11\dfrac{3}{10} - 8\dfrac{9}{10} = \boxed{} - \boxed{}$ Write mixed numbers as improper fractions.

$= \boxed{}$ Write difference of numerators over denominator.

$= \boxed{} = \boxed{}$ Subtract. Then write fraction as mixed number.

Example 4 *Simplifying Variable Expressions*

a. $\dfrac{4a}{21} + \dfrac{10a}{21} = $ [ ]   Write sum of numerators over denominator.

$= $ [ ]   Add.

$= $ [ ]   Simplify.

b. $-\dfrac{9}{5b} - \left(-\dfrac{4}{5b}\right) = $ [ ] $+$ [ ]   To subtract $-\dfrac{4}{5b}$, add [ ].

$= $ [ ]   Write sum of numerators over denominator.

$= $ [ ]   Add.

$= $ [ ]   Simplify.

✔ **Checkpoint** **Find the sum or difference.**

3. $3\dfrac{2}{11} + 5\dfrac{4}{11}$	4. $-4\dfrac{5}{13} - 3\dfrac{6}{13}$
5. $\dfrac{2a}{25} + \dfrac{8a}{25}$	6. $-\dfrac{17}{3c} - \left(-\dfrac{5}{3c}\right)$

Adding and Subtracting Unlike Fractions

Goal: Add and subtract unlike fractions.

Example 1 *Adding and Subtracting Fractions*

a. $\dfrac{7}{15} + \dfrac{1}{5} = \dfrac{7}{15} + \boxed{}$ Write $\dfrac{1}{5}$ using LCD.

$= \boxed{}$ Write sum of numerators over denominator.

$= \boxed{}$ Add.

$= \boxed{}$ Simplify.

b. $-\dfrac{2}{3} - \dfrac{3}{4} = \boxed{} - \boxed{}$ Write fractions using LCD.

$= \boxed{}$ Write difference of numerators over denominator.

$= \boxed{}$ Subtract.

$= \boxed{}$ Write fraction as a mixed number.

✔ **Checkpoint** **Find the sum or difference.**

1. $\dfrac{3}{7} + \dfrac{5}{21}$	2. $\dfrac{1}{4} - \dfrac{3}{10}$

Example 2 — Adding Mixed Numbers

$$-5\frac{1}{6} + \left(-2\frac{3}{10}\right) = \boxed{} + \boxed{}$$ Write mixed numbers as improper fractions.

$$= \boxed{} + \boxed{}$$ Write fractions using LCD.

$$= \boxed{}$$ Write sum of numerators over denominator.

$$= \boxed{} = \boxed{}$$ Add. Then write fraction as a mixed number.

Example 3 — Subtracting Mixed Numbers

You are hiking a $12\frac{1}{5}$-mile trail. You have already hiked $6\frac{1}{2}$ miles. How many more miles do you have to hike before reaching the end of the trail?

Solution

Your total hiking distance is . You have already hiked

. To find the remaining distance, subtract.

$$12\frac{1}{5} - 6\frac{1}{2} = \boxed{} - \boxed{}$$ Write mixed numbers as improper fractions.

$$= \boxed{} - \boxed{}$$ Write fractions using LCD.

$$= \boxed{}$$ Write difference of numerators over denominator.

$$= \boxed{} = \boxed{}$$ Subtract. Then write fraction as a mixed number.

Answer: You need to hike $\boxed{}$ miles.

✓ Checkpoint Find the sum or difference.

3. $4\frac{5}{6} + 2\frac{4}{9}$	4. $-2\frac{1}{3} - 3\frac{3}{7}$

Example 4 **Simplifying an Expression**

Simplify the expression $\frac{a}{4} - \frac{a}{8}$.

$\frac{a}{4} - \frac{a}{8} = \left(\frac{a}{4} \cdot \boxed{} \right) - \frac{a}{8}$ Write $\frac{a}{4}$ using LCD.

$= \boxed{} - \frac{a}{8}$ Multiply.

$= \boxed{}$ Write difference of numerators over denominator.

$= \boxed{}$ Subtract.

✓ Checkpoint Find the sum or difference.

5. $\frac{b}{3} + \frac{b}{8}$	6. $\frac{c}{5} - \frac{c}{7}$

Lesson 5.3   Adding and Subtracting Unlike Fractions   **87**

Multiplying Fractions

Goal: Multiply fractions and mixed numbers.

Multiplying Fractions

Words The product of two or more fractions is equal to the product of the numerators over the product of the denominators.

Numbers $\dfrac{3}{5} \cdot \dfrac{4}{7} = \dfrac{\boxed{}}{\boxed{}} = \dfrac{\boxed{}}{\boxed{}}$

Algebra $\dfrac{a}{b} \cdot \dfrac{c}{d} = \dfrac{\boxed{}}{\boxed{}}$, where $b \neq 0$ and $d \neq 0$

Example 1 *Multiplying Fractions*

$\dfrac{5}{12} \cdot \left(-\dfrac{3}{20} \right) = \dfrac{5}{12} \cdot \boxed{}$ Assign negative sign to numerator.

$= \boxed{}$ Use rule for multiplying fractions.

$= \dfrac{\boxed{}\ \boxed{}}{\boxed{}}$ Divide out common factors.

$ \dfrac{\boxed{}\ \boxed{}}{}$

$= \boxed{} = \boxed{}$ Multiply.

✓ **Checkpoint** Find the product.

1. $\dfrac{7}{16} \cdot \dfrac{5}{14}$	2. $\dfrac{2}{15} \cdot \left(-\dfrac{5}{18} \right)$

Example 2   *Multiplying a Mixed Number and an Integer*

Water Use The showerhead in your home uses $2\frac{1}{2}$ gallons of water per minute. If you take a 7-minute shower, how many gallons of water do you use?

Solution

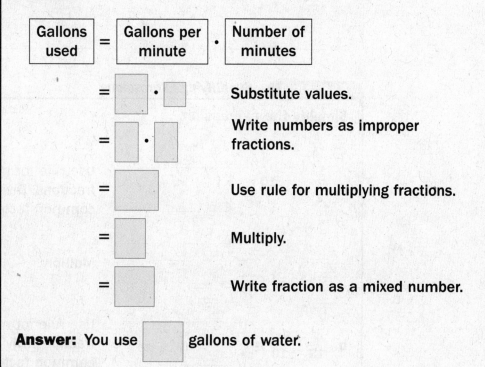

Gallons used	=	Gallons per minute	·	Number of minutes

= ☐ · ☐   Substitute values.

= ☐ · ☐   Write numbers as improper fractions.

= ☐   Use rule for multiplying fractions.

= ☐   Multiply.

= ☐   Write fraction as a mixed number.

Answer: You use ☐ gallons of water.

Example 3   *Multiplying Mixed Numbers*

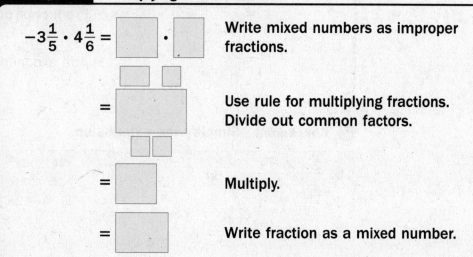

$-3\frac{1}{5} \cdot 4\frac{1}{6} =$ ☐ · ☐   Write mixed numbers as improper fractions.

$= \dfrac{\boxed{}\;\boxed{}}{\boxed{}\;\boxed{}}$ Use rule for multiplying fractions. Divide out common factors.

= ☐   Multiply.

= ☐   Write fraction as a mixed number.

Checkpoint Find the product.

3. $5\frac{2}{9} \cdot 6$	4. $-2\frac{3}{4} \cdot 5\frac{1}{3}$

Example 4 *Simplifying Expressions*

Simplify the expression.

a. $\dfrac{m}{4} \cdot \left(-\dfrac{10}{7}\right) = $ [____]   Use rule for multiplying fractions. Divide out common factor.

$= $ [____] $= $ [____]   Multiply.

b. $\dfrac{n^4}{12} \cdot \dfrac{9n^2}{10} = $ [____]   Use rule for multiplying fractions. Divide out common factor.

$= $ [____]   Product of powers property

$= $ [____]   Add exponents.

Checkpoint Simplify the expression.

5. $\dfrac{2x}{5} \cdot \dfrac{3x^2}{8}$	6. $-\dfrac{4y^3}{15} \cdot \dfrac{5y^6}{16}$

5.5 Dividing Fractions

Goal: Divide fractions and mixed numbers.

Vocabulary

Reciprocals:

Using Reciprocals to Divide

Words To divide by any nonzero number, multiply by its reciprocal.

Numbers $\dfrac{2}{9} \div \dfrac{3}{7} = \dfrac{2}{9} \cdot \boxed{} = \boxed{}$

Algebra $\dfrac{a}{b} \div \dfrac{c}{d} = \dfrac{a}{b} \cdot \boxed{} = \boxed{}$, where $b \neq 0$, $c \neq 0$, and $d \neq 0$

Example 1   *Dividing a Fraction by a Fraction*

$-\dfrac{3}{7} \div \dfrac{6}{11} = \boxed{} \cdot \boxed{}$ Multiply by reciprocal.

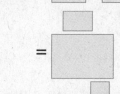 Use rule for multiplying fractions. Divide out common factor.

$= \boxed{} = \boxed{}$ Multiply.

Check: To check, multiply the quotient by the divisor to see if you get the dividend:

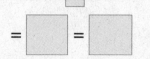

$\boxed{} \cdot \dfrac{6}{11} = \boxed{}$.

Example 2 *Dividing a Mixed Number by a Mixed Number*

$$2\frac{1}{2} \div \left(-3\frac{3}{4}\right) = \boxed{} \div \boxed{}$$ Write mixed numbers as improper fractions.

$$= \boxed{} \cdot \boxed{}$$ Multiply by reciprocal.

$$= \frac{\boxed{}\,\boxed{}}{\boxed{}\,\boxed{}}$$ Use rule for multiplying fractions. Divide out common factors.

$$= \boxed{} = \boxed{}$$ Multiply.

✓ *Checkpoint* **Find the quotient.**

1. $\dfrac{8}{21} \div \dfrac{9}{14}$	2. $-\dfrac{5}{12} \div \dfrac{5}{24}$
3. $4\dfrac{3}{5} \div 1\dfrac{7}{10}$	4. $-3\dfrac{1}{4} \div 5\dfrac{1}{2}$

Example 3   *Dividing a Whole Number by a Mixed Number*

Dogs You have two dogs that eat about $1\frac{1}{5}$ pounds of dog food per day. How many whole days will a 5-pound bag of dog food last?

Solution

Divide to find how long the bag of dog food will last.

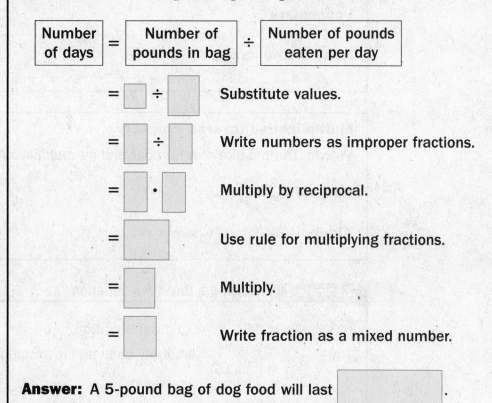

| Number of days | = | Number of pounds in bag | ÷ | Number of pounds eaten per day |

= ☐ ÷ ☐   Substitute values.

= ☐ ÷ ☐   Write numbers as improper fractions.

= ☐ · ☐   Multiply by reciprocal.

= ☐   Use rule for multiplying fractions.

= ☐   Multiply.

= ☐   Write fraction as a mixed number.

Answer: A 5-pound bag of dog food will last ☐ .

Using Multiplicative Inverses to Solve Equations

Goal: Use multiplicative inverses to solve equations.

Vocabulary

Multiplicative inverse:

Multiplicative Inverse Property

Words The product of a number and its multiplicative inverse is 1.

Numbers $\dfrac{3}{5} \cdot \dfrac{5}{3} = 1$

Algebra $\dfrac{a}{b} \cdot \dfrac{b}{a} = 1$, where $a \neq 0$, $b \neq 0$

Example 1   *Solving a One-Step Equation*

$\dfrac{3}{5}x = 15$ Original equation

$\boxed{}\left(\dfrac{3}{5}\right)x = \boxed{}(15)$ Multiply each side by multiplicative inverse of $\boxed{}$.

$\boxed{}x = \boxed{}(15)$ Multiplicative inverse property

$x = \boxed{}$ Multiply.

Answer: The solution is $\boxed{}$.

✔ *Checkpoint*   Solve the equation. Check your solution.

1. $\dfrac{6}{11}x = 18$	2. $-\dfrac{7}{13}x = 28$

Example 2 **Solving a Two-Step Equation**

$$-\frac{7}{12}x + \frac{3}{4} = \frac{1}{2}$$ Original equation

$$-\frac{7}{12}x + \frac{3}{4} - \boxed{} = \frac{1}{2} - \boxed{}$$ Subtract $\boxed{}$ from each side.

$$-\frac{7}{12}x = \boxed{} - \boxed{}$$ Write fractions using LCD.

$$-\frac{7}{12}x = \boxed{}$$ Subtract.

$$\boxed{}\left(-\frac{7}{12}\right)x = \boxed{}\left(\boxed{}\right)$$ Multiply each side by multiplicative inverse of $\boxed{}$.

$$x = \boxed{}$$ Multiply.

Example 3 **Writing and Solving a Two-Step Equation**

Tree Growth The height of a certain Norway Spruce is 10 feet. If the tree's height grows $2\frac{1}{2}$ feet per year, find how long it will take the tree to reach a height of 25 feet.

Solution

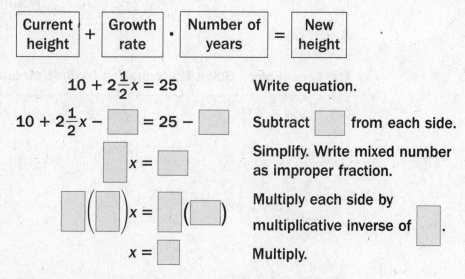

$$\boxed{\text{Current height}} + \boxed{\text{Growth rate}} \cdot \boxed{\text{Number of years}} = \boxed{\text{New height}}$$

$$10 + 2\frac{1}{2}x = 25$$ Write equation.

$$10 + 2\frac{1}{2}x - \boxed{} = 25 - \boxed{}$$ Subtract $\boxed{}$ from each side.

$$\boxed{}x = \boxed{}$$ Simplify. Write mixed number as improper fraction.

$$\boxed{}\left(\boxed{}\right)x = \boxed{}\left(\boxed{}\right)$$ Multiply each side by multiplicative inverse of $\boxed{}$.

$$x = \boxed{}$$ Multiply.

Answer: The tree will be 25 feet tall after $\boxed{}$ years.

Equations and Inequalities with Rational Numbers

Goal: Use the LCD to solve equations and inequalities.

Example 1   *Solving an Equation by Clearing Fractions*

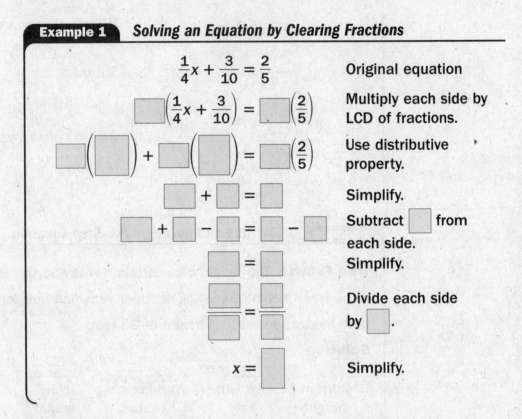

$\frac{1}{4}x + \frac{3}{10} = \frac{2}{5}$	Original equation
$\boxed{}\left(\frac{1}{4}x + \frac{3}{10}\right) = \boxed{}\left(\frac{2}{5}\right)$	Multiply each side by LCD of fractions.
$\boxed{}\left(\boxed{}\right) + \boxed{}\left(\boxed{}\right) = \boxed{}\left(\frac{2}{5}\right)$	Use distributive property.
$\boxed{} + \boxed{} = \boxed{}$	Simplify.
$\boxed{} + \boxed{} - \boxed{} = \boxed{} - \boxed{}$	Subtract $\boxed{}$ from each side.
$\boxed{} = \boxed{}$	Simplify.
$\dfrac{\boxed{}}{\boxed{}} = \dfrac{\boxed{}}{\boxed{}}$	Divide each side by $\boxed{}$.
$x = \boxed{}$	Simplify.

✔ **Checkpoint**   Solve the equation by first clearing the fractions.

1. $\frac{1}{3}x + \frac{5}{6} = \frac{7}{9}$

2. $\frac{3}{10} - \frac{7}{15}x = \frac{2}{3}$

Example 2 — Solving an Equation by Clearing Decimals

Solve the equation 2.75 = 6.15 + 0.4m.

Because the greatest number of decimal places in any of the
terms with decimals is ☐ , multiply each side of the equation
by ☐ , or ☐ .

$$2.75 = 6.15 + 0.4m$$ Original equation

$$\boxed{}(2.75) = \boxed{}(6.15 + 0.4m)$$ Multiply each side by ☐ .

$$\boxed{} = \boxed{} + \boxed{}$$ Use distributive property. Simplify.

$$\boxed{} - \boxed{} = \boxed{} + \boxed{} - \boxed{}$$ Subtract ☐ from each side.

$$\boxed{} = \boxed{}$$ Simplify.

$$\frac{\boxed{}}{\boxed{}} = \frac{\boxed{}}{\boxed{}}$$ Divide each side by ☐ .

$$\boxed{} = m$$ Simplify.

Example 3   *Solving an Inequality with Fractions*

Geometry Describe the possible values of x if the area of the rectangle is at least 24 square inches.

6

$\frac{2}{5}x + 2$

Solution

Length	·	Width	≥	Area

$\boxed{} \cdot \boxed{\ } \geq \boxed{\ }$ Substitute.

$\boxed{\ } + \boxed{\ } \geq \boxed{\ }$ Use distributive property.

$\boxed{\ } + \boxed{\ } - \boxed{\ } \geq \boxed{\ } - \boxed{\ }$ Subtract $\boxed{\ }$ from each side.

$\boxed{\ } \geq \boxed{\ }$ Simplify.

$\boxed{\ } \left(\boxed{\ } \right) \geq \boxed{\ } \left(\boxed{\ } \right)$ Multiply each side by multiplicative inverse of $\boxed{\ }$.

$\boxed{\ } \geq \boxed{\ }$ Simplify.

Answer: The possible values of x are $\boxed{}$.

Example 4 **Solving an Inequality by Clearing Fractions**

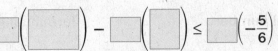

$$-\frac{1}{6}m - \frac{5}{12} \leq -\frac{5}{6}$$ Original inequality

$\left(-\dfrac{1}{6}m - \dfrac{5}{12}\right) \leq$ 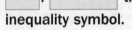$\left(-\dfrac{5}{6}\right)$ Multiply each side by LCD of fractions.

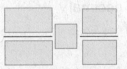 $\leq$ $\left(-\dfrac{5}{6}\right)$ Use distributive property.

$\boxed{} - \boxed{} \leq \boxed{}$ Simplify.

$\boxed{} - \boxed{} + \boxed{} \leq \boxed{} + \boxed{}$ Add $\boxed{}$ to each side.

$\boxed{} \leq \boxed{}$ Simplify.

  Divide each side by $\boxed{}$. $\boxed{}$ the inequality symbol.

$m \boxed{} \boxed{}$ Simplify.

✔ *Checkpoint* **Solve the inequality by first clearing the fractions.**

3. $\dfrac{4}{11}x + 1 < \dfrac{2}{3}$

4. $\dfrac{3}{7}x + \dfrac{1}{4} < \dfrac{1}{2}$

Words to Review

Give an example of the vocabulary word.

Rational number

Terminating decimal

Repeating decimal

Reciprocal

Multiplicative inverse

Review your notes and Chapter 5 by using the Chapter Review on pages 258–261 of your textbook.

6.1 Ratios and Rates

Goal: Find ratios and unit rates.

Vocabulary

Ratio:

Equivalent ratios:

Writing Ratios

You can write the ratio of two quantities, a and b, where b is not equal to 0, in three ways.

$$a \text{ to } b \qquad a : b \qquad \frac{a}{b}$$

Each ratio is read "the ratio of a to b." You should write the ratio in simplest form.

Example 1   *Writing Ratios*

In a recent baseball season, the Anaheim Angels played 81 home games. Anaheim won 54 of those games and lost 27. Write the ratio in three ways.

a. The number of losses to the number of wins

b. The number of losses to the number of games

Solution

a. ⬚ = ⬚ = ⬚

b. ⬚ = ⬚ = ⬚

Three ways to write the ratio are ⬚, ⬚, and ⬚.

Three ways to write the ratio are ⬚, ⬚, and ⬚.

✔ **Checkpoint**

1. Use the information given in Example 1. Compare the number of wins to the number of games using a ratio. Write the ratio in three ways.

Example 2   *Finding a Unit Rate*

Vacation On the first day of a family vacation, you and your family drive 392 miles. The amount of gasoline used is 16 gallons. What is the average mileage per gallon of gasoline?

Solution

First, write a rate comparing the [ ] to the [ ]. Then write the rate so the denominator is [ ].

[ ] = [ ]   Divide numerator and denominator by [ ].

= [ ]   Simplify.

Answer: The average mileage per gallon of gasoline is [ ].

✔ **Checkpoint**   Find the unit rate.

2. $\dfrac{220 \text{ mi}}{4 \text{ h}}$

3. $\dfrac{\$115}{5 \text{ people}}$

Example 3 — Writing an Equivalent Rate

Water The amount of water used in a certain home is 728 gallons per week. Write this rate in gallons per day.

Solution

To convert from gallons per week to gallons per day, multiply the rate by a conversion factor. There are 7 days in 1 week, so $\boxed{}$ = 1.

$$\frac{728 \text{ gal}}{1 \text{ week}} = \boxed{} \cdot \boxed{} \qquad \text{Multiply rate by conversion factor.}$$

$$= \boxed{} \cdot \boxed{} \qquad \text{Divide out common factor and unit.}$$

$$= \boxed{} \qquad \text{Simplify.}$$

Answer: The amount of water used is $\boxed{}$.

Example 4 — Using Equivalent Rates

Weather Lightning strikes occur about 100 times per second around the world. About how many lightning strikes occur in 3 minutes?

Solution

1. Express the rate 100 times per second in times per minute.

$$\frac{100 \text{ times}}{1 \text{ sec}} = \boxed{} \cdot \boxed{} \qquad \text{Multiply by conversion factor. Divide out common unit.}$$

$$= \boxed{} \qquad \text{Simplify.}$$

2. Find the number of times lightning strikes occur around the world in 3 minutes.

Number of times = Rate · Time

$$= \boxed{} \cdot \boxed{} \qquad \text{Substitute values. Divide out common unit.}$$

$$= \boxed{} \qquad \text{Multiply.}$$

Answer: In 3 minutes, about $\boxed{}$ lightning strikes occur around the world.

6.2 Writing and Solving Proportions

Goal: Write and solve proportions.

Proportions

Words A proportion is an equation that states that two ratios are equivalent.

Numbers $\dfrac{2}{3} = \dfrac{8}{12}$

Algebra $\dfrac{a}{b} = \dfrac{c}{d}$, where $b \neq 0$ and $d \neq 0$

Example 1 *Solving a Proportion Using Equivalent Ratios*

Solve the proportion $\dfrac{3}{5} = \dfrac{x}{20}$.

1. Compare denominators.

$$\dfrac{3}{5} \; \times \; \boxed{} \; \longrightarrow \; \dfrac{x}{20}$$

2. Find x.

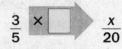

Answer: Because $3 \times \boxed{} = \boxed{}$, $x = \boxed{}$.

✔ **Checkpoint** Use equivalent ratios to solve the proportion.

1. $\dfrac{2}{9} = \dfrac{x}{27}$	**2.** $\dfrac{5}{6} = \dfrac{x}{36}$

Example 2 *Solving a Proportion Using Algebra*

Solve the proportion $\dfrac{x}{15} = \dfrac{2}{5}$. Check your answer.

$$\dfrac{x}{15} = \dfrac{2}{5}$$ Write original proportion.

$\boxed{} \cdot \dfrac{x}{15} = \boxed{} \cdot \dfrac{2}{5}$ Multiply each side by $\boxed{}$.

$x = \boxed{}$ Simplify.

$x = \boxed{}$ Divide.

Check: $\dfrac{x}{15} = \dfrac{2}{5}$ Write original proportion.

$\dfrac{\boxed{}}{15} \stackrel{?}{=} \dfrac{2}{5}$ Substitute $\boxed{}$ for x.

$\boxed{}\boxed{} \dfrac{2}{5}$ Simplify. $\boxed{}$

✔ *Checkpoint*   **Use algebra to solve the proportion.**

3. $\dfrac{3}{7} = \dfrac{x}{28}$	**4.** $\dfrac{8}{11} = \dfrac{x}{55}$
5. $\dfrac{x}{8} = \dfrac{49}{56}$	**6.** $\dfrac{x}{6} = \dfrac{14}{3}$

Example 3 **Writing and Solving a Proportion**

Maple Syrup The sap of maple trees is used to make maple syrup. To make 1 gallon of maple syrup takes 40 gallons of sap. Write and solve a proportion to find the number of gallons of maple syrup that can be made from 1520 gallons of sap.

Solution

First, write a proportion involving two ratios that compare the number of gallons of maple syrup to the number of gallons of sap.

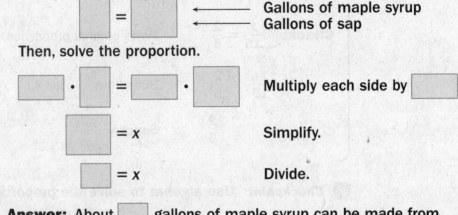

Then, solve the proportion.

Multiply each side by ☐.

☐ = x   Simplify.

☐ = x   Divide.

Answer: About ☐ gallons of maple syrup can be made from 1520 gallons of sap.

✔ **Checkpoint**

7. Use the information in Example 3. Write and solve a proportion to find the number of gallons of maple syrup that can be made from 1360 gallons of sap.

6.3 Solving Proportions Using Cross Products

Goal: Solve proportions using cross products.

Vocabulary

Cross product:

Example 1 *Determining if Ratios Form a Proportion*

Tell whether the ratios form a proportion.

a. $\dfrac{4}{26}, \dfrac{8}{42}$

b. $\dfrac{12}{21}, \dfrac{20}{35}$

Solution

a.

$$\dfrac{4}{26} \overset{?}{=} \dfrac{8}{42}$$ Write proportion.

[ ] · [ ] $\overset{?}{=}$ [ ] · [ ]   Form cross products.

[ ] [ ] [ ]   Multiply.

Answer: The ratios [   ] a proportion.

b.

$$\dfrac{12}{21} \overset{?}{=} \dfrac{20}{35}$$ Write proportion.

[ ] · [ ] $\overset{?}{=}$ [ ] · [ ]   Form cross products.

[ ] [ ] [ ]   Multiply.

Answer: The ratios [   ] a proportion.

Cross Products Property

Words The cross products of a proportion are equal.

Numbers Given that $\dfrac{2}{5} = \dfrac{6}{15}$, you know that [   ] = [   ].

Algebra If $\dfrac{a}{b} = \dfrac{c}{d}$, where $b \neq 0$ and $d \neq 0$, then [   ] = [   ].

Example 2 **Writing and Solving a Proportion**

Earnings You earn $68 mowing 4 lawns. How much would you earn if you mowed 7 lawns?

Solution

$$\boxed{} = \boxed{} \quad \longleftarrow \text{Money earned}$$
$$\quad\quad\quad\quad\quad \longleftarrow \text{Lawns mowed}$$

$$\boxed{} \cdot \boxed{} = \boxed{} \cdot \boxed{} \quad \text{Cross products property}$$

$$\boxed{} = \boxed{} \quad \text{Multiply.}$$

$$\boxed{} = \boxed{} \quad \text{Divide each side by } \boxed{}.$$

$$\boxed{} = x \quad \text{Simplify.}$$

Answer: If you mowed 7 lawns, you would earn $\boxed{}$.

✔ **Checkpoint** **Tell whether the ratios form a proportion.**

1. $\dfrac{9}{39} = \dfrac{15}{65}$	2. $\dfrac{12}{45} = \dfrac{6}{28}$

Use the cross products property to solve the proportion.

3. $\dfrac{14}{42} = \dfrac{x}{6}$	4. $\dfrac{4}{9} = \dfrac{16}{x}$

6.4 Similar and Congruent Figures

Goal: Identify similar and congruent figures.

Vocabulary

Similar
figures:

Corresponding
parts:

Congruent
figures:

When naming similar figures, list the letters of the corresponding vertices in the same order. For the diagram at the right, it is not correct to say $\triangle CBA \sim \triangle EFD$, because $\angle C$ and $\angle E$ are not corresponding angles.

Properties of Similar Figures

$\triangle ABC \sim \triangle DEF$

The symbol $\sim$ indicates that two figures are similar.

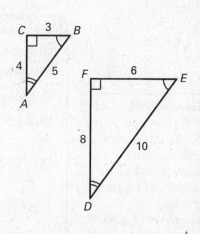

1. Corresponding angles of similar figures are congruent.

   $\angle A \cong \angle D,\ \angle B \cong \angle E,\ \angle C \cong \angle F$

2. The ratios of the lengths of corresponding sides of similar figures are equal.

   $$\frac{AB}{DE} = \frac{BC}{EF} = \frac{AC}{DF} = \frac{1}{2}$$

Given △XYZ ~ △UVW, name the corresponding angles and the corresponding sides.

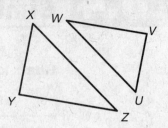

Solution

Corresponding angles:

Corresponding sides:

✔ *Checkpoint*

1. Given *STUV* ~ *WXYZ*, name the corresponding angles and the corresponding sides.

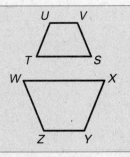

Example 2   *Finding the Ratio of Corresponding Side Lengths*

Given *ABCD* ~ *QRST*, find the ratio of the lengths of the corresponding sides of *ABCD* to *QRST*.

Write a ratio comparing the lengths of a pair of corresponding sides. Then substitute the lengths of the sides and simplify.

$$\frac{AD}{QT} = \boxed{} = \boxed{}$$

Because all the ratios of the lengths of corresponding sides of the figure in Example 2 are equal, you can use any pair of lengths of corresponding sides to write the ratio. To check the solution, choose another pair of lengths of corresponding sides.

Answer: The ratio of the lengths of the corresponding sides is $\boxed{}$.

2. Given *FGHJ* ~ *KLMN*, find the ratio of the lengths of the corresponding sides of *FGHJ* to *KLMN*.

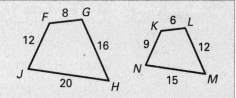

Example 3 **Finding Measures of Congruent Figures**

Given *DEFG* ≅ *KLMN*, find the indicated measure.

a. *KL*   **b.** ∠*L*

Solution

Because the quadrilaterals are congruent, the corresponding angles are congruent and the corresponding sides are congruent.

a. $\overline{KL}$ ≅ [   ]. So, *KL* = [   ] = [   ]

b. ∠*L* ≅ [   ]. So, *m*∠*L* = [   ] = [   ]

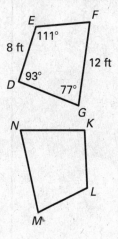

✔ **Checkpoint**

3. Given △*ABC* ≅ △*LMK*, find *m*∠*L*.

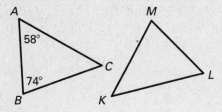

Similarity and Measurement

Goal: Find unknown side lengths of similar figures.

Example 1 *Finding an Unknown Side Length in Similar Figures*

Given *RSTV* ~ *WXYZ*, find *VR*.

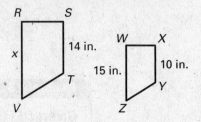

Solution

Use the ratios of the lengths of corresponding sides to write a proportion involving the unknown length, *VR*.

$$\frac{XY}{ST} = \boxed{}$$ Write proportion involving *VR*.

$$\boxed{} = \boxed{}$$ Substitute.

$$\boxed{} \cdot \boxed{} = \boxed{} \cdot \boxed{}$$ Cross products property

$$\boxed{} = \boxed{}$$ Multiply.

$$x = \boxed{}$$ Divide each side by $\boxed{}$.

Answer: The length of $\overline{VR}$ is $\boxed{}$ inches.

✓ *Checkpoint*

1. Given △*PQR* ~ △*VTS*, find *TS*.

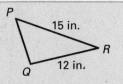

Example 2 — Using Indirect Measurement

Height At a certain time of day, a person who is 6 feet tall casts a 3-foot shadow. At the same time, a tree casts an 11-foot shadow. The triangles formed are similar. Find the height of the tree.

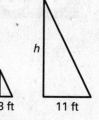

Solution

Write and solve a proportion to find the height h of the tree.

$$\dfrac{\text{Height of tree}}{\text{Height of person}} = \boxed{}$$

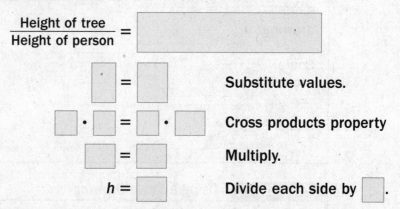

$$\boxed{} = \boxed{} \qquad \text{Substitute values.}$$

$$\boxed{} \cdot \boxed{} = \boxed{} \cdot \boxed{} \qquad \text{Cross products property}$$

$$\boxed{} = \boxed{} \qquad \text{Multiply.}$$

$$h = \boxed{} \qquad \text{Divide each side by } \boxed{}.$$

Answer: The tree has a height of $\boxed{}$ feet.

Example 3 — Using Algebra and Similar Triangles

Given $\triangle ABC \sim \triangle DEC$, find BE.

To find BE, write and solve a proportion.

Figure labels: 30 in. (CE), E, x, B, 16 in. (ED), 24 in. (BA), D, A, C

$$\dfrac{AB}{DE} = \boxed{} \qquad \text{Write proportion.}$$

$$\boxed{} = \boxed{} \qquad \text{Use fact that } BC = \boxed{}.$$

$$\boxed{} = \boxed{} \qquad \text{Substitute.}$$

$$\boxed{} = \boxed{} \qquad \text{Cross products property}$$

$$\boxed{} = \boxed{} \qquad \text{Multiply.}$$

$$\boxed{} = \boxed{} \qquad \text{Subtract } \boxed{} \text{ from each side.}$$

$$\boxed{} = x \qquad \text{Divide each side by } \boxed{}.$$

Answer: The length of $\overline{BE}$ is $\boxed{}$ inches.

6.6 Scale Drawings

Goal: Use proportions with scale drawings.

Vocabulary

Scale
drawing:

Scale
model:

Scale:

Example 1 *Using a Scale Drawing*

On a map, the distance between two cities is 3 inches. What is the actual distance (in miles) between the two cities if the map's scale is 1 in. : 125 mi?

Solution

Let x represent the actual distance (in miles) between the two cities. The ratio of the map distance between the two cities to the actual distance x is equal to the scale of the map. Write and solve a proportion using this relationship.

$$\boxed{} = \boxed{} \quad \longleftarrow \quad \text{Map distance} \\ \longleftarrow \quad \text{Actual distance}$$

$$\boxed{} = \boxed{} \quad \text{Cross products property}$$

$$x = \boxed{} \quad \text{Multiply.}$$

Answer: The actual distance is $\boxed{}$.

✔ *Checkpoint*

1. On a map, the distance between two cities is 4 inches. What is the actual distance (in miles) between the two cities if the map's scale is 1 in. : 80 mi?

Example 2   *Finding the Scale of a Drawing*

Architecture In a scale drawing, a wall is 2 inches long. The actual wall is 12 feet long. Find the scale of the drawing.

Solution

Write a ratio using corresponding side lengths of the scale drawing and the actual wall. Then simplify the ratio so that the numerator is ☐.

$$\frac{2 \text{ in.}}{12 \text{ ft}} \longleftarrow \text{Length of wall in scale drawing}$$
$$\phantom{\frac{2 \text{ in.}}{12 \text{ ft}}} \longleftarrow \text{Length of actual wall}$$

$$\frac{2 \text{ in.}}{12 \text{ ft}} = \boxed{} \qquad \text{Simplify.}$$

Answer: The drawing's scale is ☐.

Example 3   *Finding a Dimension of a Scale Model*

A model of the Sears Tower in Chicago has a scale of 1 : 103. The height of the Sears Tower's observation deck is about 412 meters. Find the height of the observation deck of the model.

Solution

Write a proportion using the scale.

$$\boxed{} = \boxed{} \longleftarrow \text{Dimension of model}$$
$$ \longleftarrow \text{Dimension of Sears Tower}$$

$$\boxed{} = \boxed{} \qquad \text{Cross products property}$$

$$\boxed{} = x \qquad \text{Divide each side by } \boxed{}.$$

Answer: The height of the model's observation deck is ☐.

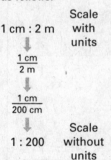

The scale of a scale drawing or scale model can be written without units if the measurements have the same unit. For example, the scale 1 cm : 2 m can be written without units as follows.

1 cm : 2 m   — Scale with units

$$\frac{1 \text{ cm}}{2 \text{ m}}$$

$$\frac{1 \text{ cm}}{200 \text{ cm}}$$

1 : 200   — Scale without units

✔ *Checkpoint*

2. The height of one antenna on the Sears Tower is about 521.1 meters. Find the height of the antenna on the model to the nearest tenth of a meter.

6.7 Probability and Odds

Goal: Find probabilities.

Vocabulary

Outcomes:

Event:

Favorable outcomes:

Probability:

Theoretical probability:

Experimental probability:

Odds in favor:

Odds against:

Probability of an Event

The probability of an event when all outcomes are equally likely is:

$$P(\text{event}) = \frac{\text{Number of favorable outcomes}}{\text{Number of possible outcomes}}$$

Example 1   *Finding a Probability*

Suppose you roll a number cube. What is the probability that you roll an odd number?

Solution

Rolls of ⬚⬚⬚⬚ are odd, so there are ⬚ favorable outcomes. There are ⬚ possible outcomes.

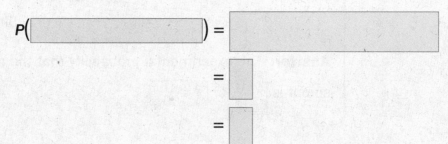

$$P\left(\right) = $$

$$= $$

$$= $$

✔ **Checkpoint**

1. Suppose you roll a number cube. What is the probability that you roll a number less than 5?

2. Suppose you roll a number cube. What is the probability that you roll a number that is a multiple of 3?

Experimental Probability

The experimental probability of an event is:

$$P(\text{event}) = \frac{\text{Number of successes}}{\text{Number of trials}}$$

Example 2   *Finding Experimental Probability*

You plant 32 seeds of a certain flower and 18 of them sprout. Find the experimental probability that the next flower seed planted will sprout.

Solution

$P(\text{flower seed will sprout}) = \boxed{}$ ⟵ Number of successes
⟵ Number of trials

$= \boxed{}$ Simplify.

Answer: The experimental probability that the next flower seed will sprout is $\boxed{}$, or $\boxed{}$.

Example 3   *Finding the Odds*

Suppose you randomly choose a number between 1 and 16.

a. What are the odds in favor of choosing a prime number?

b. What are the odds against choosing a prime number?

Solution

a. There are $\boxed{}$ favorable outcomes ($\boxed{}$) and

$16 - \boxed{} = \boxed{}$ unfavorable outcomes.

$$\text{Odds in favor} = \frac{\text{Number of favorable outcomes}}{\text{Number of unfavorable outcomes}} = \boxed{} = \boxed{}$$

The odds are $\boxed{}$, or $\boxed{}$ to $\boxed{}$, that you choose a prime number.

b. The odds against choose a prime number are $\boxed{}$, or $\boxed{}$ to $\boxed{}$.

6.8 The Counting Principle

Goal: Use the counting principle to find probabilities.

Vocabulary

Tree diagram:

Counting principle:

Example 1 | *Making a Tree Diagram*

At a picnic lunch, you can choose one sandwich and one salad. The choices include the following: veggie burger, hamburger, tuna sandwich, garden salad, and fruit salad. How many different picnic lunches are possible?

Solution

To count the number of possible picnic lunches, you can make a tree diagram.

List the sandwiches.	List the salads for each sandwich.	List the possibilities for each picnic lunch.

Answer: [ ] different picnic lunches are possible.

1. Suppose for each picnic lunch in Example 1 you also get to choose one fruit. The choices include the following: apple, banana, orange, and grapefruit. Copy the tree diagram in Example 1 and add the new choices. How many possible picnic lunch choices are there?

The Counting Principle

If one event can occur in m ways, and for each of these ways a second event can occur in n ways, then the number of ways that the two events can occur together is $m \cdot n$.

The counting principle can be extended to three or more events.

Example 2   Use the Counting Principle

You roll a number cube and randomly draw a marble from a bag. There is one marble for each of the following colors: red, blue, green, and yellow. Use the counting principle to find the number of different outcomes that are possible.

Number of outcomes for the number cube		Number of outcomes for the marble		Total number of possible outcomes
☐	•	☐	=	☐

Answer: There are ☐ different possible outcomes.

2. You roll a number cube, randomly draw a marble from a bag, and flip a coin. There is one marble for each of the following colors: red, blue, and yellow. Use the counting principle to find the number of different outcomes that are possible.

Example 3   *Finding a Probability*

Car Security The access code for a car's security system consists of 4 digits. You randomly enter 4 digits. What is the probability that you choose the correct code?

Solution

First find the number of different codes.

$$\boxed{} = \boxed{} \qquad \text{Use the counting principle.}$$

Then find the probability that you choose the correct code.

$$P(\text{correct code}) = \boxed{}$$

Answer: The probability that you choose the correct code is $\boxed{}$.

✓ **Checkpoint**

3. Your computer password has 2 lowercase letters followed by 6 digits. Your friend randomly chooses 2 lowercase letters and 6 digits. Use a calculator to find the probability that your friend chooses your password.

Words to Review

Give an example of the vocabulary word.

Ratio

Equivalent ratios

Proportion

Cross products

Similar figures

Corresponding parts

Congruent figures

Scale drawing

Scale model

Scale

Outcomes

Event

Favorable outcomes

Probability

Theoretical probability

Experimental probability

Odds in favor

Odds against

Tree diagram

Counting principle

Review your notes and Chapter 6 by using the Chapter Review on pages 318–321 of your textbook.

7.1 Percents and Fractions

Goal: Use a fraction to find the percent of a number.

Vocabulary

Percent:

Writing Percents

Words In the area model shown, 85 of the 100 squares are shaded. You can say that 85 percent of the squares are shaded.

Numbers $\dfrac{85}{100} = 85\%$

Algebra $\dfrac{p}{100} = p\%$

Example 1 *Writing Percents as Fractions, Fractions as Percents*

Write 31% and 60% as fractions in simplest form.

a. $31\% = \boxed{}$ b. $60\% = \boxed{} = \boxed{}$

Write $\dfrac{3}{10}$ and $\dfrac{4}{5}$ as percents.

a. $\dfrac{3}{10} = \dfrac{3 \cdot \boxed{}}{10 \cdot \boxed{}} = \boxed{} = \boxed{}$

b. $\dfrac{4}{5} = \dfrac{4 \cdot \boxed{}}{5 \cdot \boxed{}} = \boxed{} = \boxed{}$

Write the percent as a fraction in simplest form, or write the fraction as a percent.

1. 73%	**2.** 40%	**3.** $\frac{9}{10}$	**4.** $\frac{4}{25}$

Example 2   *Writing a Probability as a Percent*

Random Number A computer randomly generates an integer from 1 to 10. Find the probability that 8 is the integer generated.

Solution

There are ☐ possible outcomes, and ☐ outcome is favorable.

$P(8) =$ ☐   Write probability as a fraction.

$ =$ ☐   Write fraction as percent.

Answer: The probability that 8 is the integer generated is ☐.

✓ **Checkpoint** A computer randomly generates an integer from 1 to 10. Find the probability of the given event. Write your answer as a percent.

5. $P(2)$	**6.** P(prime number)

Example 3   *Finding a Percent of a Number*

Crackers In a survey of 85 people, 20% of them said they usually eat crackers with soup. How many people in the survey said they usually eat crackers with soup?

Solution

To find 20% of 85, use the fact that 20% = ☐ . Then multiply.

20% of 85 = ☐ · ☐   Write percent as a fraction.

= ☐   Simplify.

Answer: ☐ people said they usually eat crackers with soup.

✓ *Checkpoint*   **Find the percent of the number.**

7. 30% of 80	8. 60% of 105

Percents and Proportions

Goal: Use proportions to solve percent problems.

Solving Percent Problems

You can represent "*a* is *p* percent of *b*" using the proportion

$$\frac{a}{b} = \frac{p}{100}$$

where *a* is a part of the base *b* and *p*%, or $\frac{p}{100}$, is the percent.

Example 1   *Finding a Percent*

What percent of 9 is 5?

$$\frac{a}{b} = \frac{p}{100}$$ Write proportion.

$$\boxed{} = \frac{p}{100}$$ Substitute for *a* and for *b*.

$$\boxed{} \cdot \frac{5}{9} = \boxed{} \cdot \frac{p}{100}$$ Multiply each side by $\boxed{}$.

$$\boxed{} = p$$ Simplify.

Answer: 5 is $\boxed{}$ % of 9.

✔ *Checkpoint*   Use a proportion to answer the question.

1. What percent of 28 is 4?	**2.** What percent of 80 is 30?

Example 2   *Finding a Part of a Base*

What number is 15% of 300?

$$\frac{a}{b} = \frac{p}{100}$$ Write proportion.

$$\frac{a}{\boxed{}} = \frac{\boxed{}}{100}$$ Substitute for *b* and for *p.*

$$\boxed{} \cdot \frac{a}{\boxed{}} = \boxed{} \cdot \frac{\boxed{}}{100}$$ Multiply each side by $\boxed{}$.

$$a = \boxed{}$$ Simplify.

Answer: $\boxed{}$ is 15% of 300.

Example 3   *Finding a Base*

Student Council Election You receive 189 votes, or 45%, of the votes in the student council election. How many students voted?

Solution

189 is a part of the total number of voters, which is the base.

$$\frac{a}{b} = \frac{p}{100}$$ Write proportion.

$$\frac{\boxed{}}{b} = \frac{\boxed{}}{100}$$ Substitute for *a* and for *p.*

$$\boxed{} \cdot \boxed{} = \boxed{} \cdot \boxed{}$$ Cross products property

$$\boxed{} = \boxed{}$$ Multiply.

$$\boxed{} = b$$ Divide each side by $\boxed{}$.

Answer: $\boxed{}$ students voted in the election.

 Checkpoint   Use a proportion to answer the question.

3. What number is 62% of 200?	4. 117 is 78% of what number?

7.3 Percents and Decimals

Goal: Use decimals to solve percent problems.

Percents and Decimals

- To write a decimal as a percent, move the decimal point two places to the [ ] and [ ].

- To write a percent as a decimal, move the decimal point two places to the [ ] and [ ].

Example 1 *Writing Decimals as Percents*

Write 0.17, 2, and 3.2 as percents.

a. 0.17 = 0.17

= [ ]

b. 2 = 2.00

= [ ]

c. 3.2 = 3.20

= [ ]

Example 2 *Writing Percents as Decimals*

Write 63%, 0.7%, and 129% as decimals.

a. 63% = 63%

= [ ]

b. 0.7% = 00.7%

= [ ]

c. 129% = 129%

= [ ]

✓ *Checkpoint* Write the decimal as a percent or the percent as a decimal.

1. 0.54	2. 4	3. 1.75	4. 0.03
5. 41%	6. 147%	7. 9%	8. 12.5%

Example 3   *Writing Fractions as Percents*

Write $\frac{4}{9}$ and $\frac{7}{4}$ as percents.

a. $\frac{4}{9} =$ ☐   Write fraction as a decimal.

= ☐   Write decimal as a percent.

b. $\frac{7}{4} =$ ☐   Write fraction as a decimal.

= ☐   Write decimal as a percent.

✔ *Checkpoint* **Write the fraction as a percent.**

9. $\frac{5}{8}$	10. $\frac{8}{9}$	11. $\frac{11}{5}$	12. $\frac{13}{6}$

Example 4   *Finding a Percent of a Number*

Day of Dread In a survey of 1300 adults, 18% said the day they dread the most is Monday. How many adults chose Monday?

Solution

Find 18% of 1300.

18% of 1300 = ☐ · 1300   Write percent as decimal.

= ☐   Multiply.

Answer: The number of adults that chose Monday is ☐.

✔ *Checkpoint* **Find the percent of the number.**

13. 25% of 76	14. 110% of 65	15. 0.7% of 500

7.4 The Percent Equation

Goal: Use equations to solve percent problems.

The Percent Equation

You can represent "a is p percent of b" using the equation

$a = p\% \cdot b$

where a is a part of the base b and $p\%$ is the percent.

Example 1   *Finding a Part of a Base*

In a newspaper's survey, 1100 adults were asked to name their favorite condiment. The most frequent response was ketchup, which was given by 47% of the adults. How many adults chose ketchup?

Solution

To find how many adults chose ketchup as their favorite condiment, use the percent equation.

$a = p\% \cdot b$ Write percent equation.

$= \boxed{} \cdot \boxed{}$ Substitute for p and for b.

$= \boxed{} \cdot \boxed{}$ Write percent as a decimal.

$= \boxed{}$ Multiply.

Answer: The number of adults who chose ketchup as their favorite condiment was $\boxed{}$.

✓ *Checkpoint*   Use the percent equation to answer the question.

1. What number is 15% of 60?	2. What number is 78% of 105?

Example 2 *Finding a Commission*

Commission A sales person earns 5.5% commission on every car sold. The sales person sells a car for $41,200. What is the commission?

Solution

$a = p\% \cdot b$ Write percent equation.

$= \boxed{} \cdot \boxed{}$ Substitute for p and for b.

$= \boxed{} \cdot \boxed{}$ Write percent as decimal.

$= \boxed{}$ Multiply.

Answer: The commission is $\$\boxed{}$.

✓ *Checkpoint*

3. In Example 2, find the commission if a car is sold for $45,000.

Example 3 *Finding a Percent*

What percent of 24 is 84?

$a = p\% \cdot b$ Write percent equation.

$\boxed{} = p\% \cdot \boxed{}$ Substitute for a and for b.

$\boxed{} = p\%$ Divide each side by $\boxed{}$.

$\boxed{} = p\%$ Write decimal as a percent.

Answer: 84 is $\boxed{}$ % of 24.

✓ Checkpoint Use the percent equation to answer the question.

4. What percent of 15 is 21?	5. What percent of 72 is 45?

Example 4 **Finding a Base**

Football Your friend paid $48 for a ticket to a professional football game. This amount was 64% of the total amount your friend spent at the game. How much money did your friend spend?

Solution

$a = p\% \cdot b$ Write percent equation.

$\boxed{} = \boxed{}\% \cdot b$ Substitute for a and for p.

$\boxed{} = \boxed{} \cdot b$ Write percent as decimal.

$\boxed{} = b$ Divide each side by $\boxed{}$.

Answer: Your friend spent $\$\boxed{}$ at the game.

✓ Checkpoint Use the percent equation to answer the question.

6. 33 is 30% of what number?	7. 90 is 37.5% of what number?

7.5 Percent of Change

Goal: Find a percent of change in a quantity.

Vocabulary

Percent
of change:

Percent
of increase:

Percent
of decrease:

Percent of Change

The percent of change is the ratio of the amount of increase or decrease to the original amount.

$$\text{Percent of change, } p\% = \frac{\text{Amount of increase or decrease}}{\text{Original amount}}$$

Example 1   *Finding a Percent of Increase*

Enrollment A school had 720 students enrolled last year. This year, 745 students are enrolled. By about what percent did the number of students change from last year to this year?

$p\% = \dfrac{\text{Amount of increase}}{\text{Original amount}}$ Write formula for percent of increase.

$=$ [ ]   Substitute.

$=$ [ ]   Subtract.

$\approx$ [ ] $=$ [ ]   Divide. Then write decimal as a percent.

Answer: The number of students increased by about [ ]%.

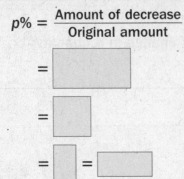

Example 2 — Finding a Percent of Decrease

Find the percent of decrease from 576 to 216.

$p\% = \dfrac{\text{Amount of decrease}}{\text{Original amount}}$ Write formula for percent of decrease.

$= \boxed{}$ Substitute.

$= \boxed{}$ Subtract.

$= \boxed{} = \boxed{}$ Simplify fraction. Then write the fraction as a percent.

Answer: The percent of decrease is $\boxed{}$ %.

Example 3 — Using a Percent of Increase

Ticket Prices A professional baseball team announces that the average ticket price to one of their games will be 8% more than last year. If the average price of a ticket was $12 last year, how much will the average ticket cost this year?

Solution

To find the average ticket cost this year, you need to increase the average ticket cost last year by 8%.

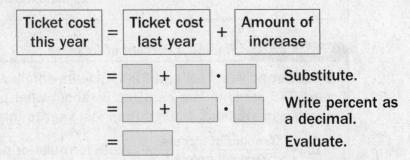

| Ticket cost this year | = | Ticket cost last year | + | Amount of increase |

$= \boxed{} + \boxed{} \cdot \boxed{}$ Substitute.

$= \boxed{} + \boxed{} \cdot \boxed{}$ Write percent as a decimal.

$= \boxed{}$ Evaluate.

Answer: This year, the average ticket will cost $\boxed{}$.

Example 4   *Finding a New Amount*

Tuna In 1990, the average price per pound of light chunk tuna was $2.11. By 2001, the average price per pound had decreased by 7.1%. What was the average price per pound in 2001?

Solution

Price in 2001 = Price in 1990 · (100% − p%)

$$= \boxed{} \cdot \left(100\% - \boxed{}\%\right) \quad \text{Substitute.}$$

$$= \boxed{} \cdot \boxed{} \quad \text{Subtract percents.}$$

$$= \boxed{} \cdot \boxed{} \quad \text{Write percent as a decimal.}$$

$$= \boxed{} \quad \text{Multiply.}$$

Answer: The average price per pound in 2001 was about $\boxed{}$.

> To find a new amount, do one of the following.
> · For a p% increase, multiply the original amount by (100% + p%).
> · For a p% decrease, multiply the original amount by (100% − p%).

✔ *Checkpoint*   **Find the percent of increase.**

1. Original: 25 New: 31	2. Original: 150 New: 195

Find the new amount.

3. Increase 54 by 25%.	4. Decrease 78 by 40%.

7.6 Percent Applications

Goal: Find markups, discounts, sales tax, and tips.

Vocabulary

Markup: [   ]

Discount: [   ]

Example 1   *Finding a Retail Price*

Pillows A store buys decorative pillows from a manufacturer for $2 each. The store marks up the price by 400%. What is the retail price?

Solution

Method 1 Add the markup to the wholesale price.

Retail price = Wholesale price + Markup

$$= \boxed{} + \boxed{} \cdot \boxed{} \qquad \text{Substitute.}$$

$$= \boxed{} + \boxed{} \cdot \boxed{} \qquad \text{Write } \boxed{} \text{ as a decimal.}$$

$$= \boxed{} + \boxed{} \qquad \text{Multiply.}$$

$$= \boxed{} \qquad \text{Add.}$$

Method 2 Multiply the wholesale price by (100% + Markup percent).

Retail price = Wholesale price · (100% + Markup percent)

$$= \boxed{} \cdot \left(100\% + \boxed{}\right) \qquad \text{Substitute.}$$

$$= \boxed{} \cdot \boxed{} \qquad \text{Add percents.}$$

$$= \boxed{} \cdot \boxed{} \qquad \text{Write } \boxed{} \text{ as a decimal.}$$

$$= \boxed{} \qquad \text{Multiply.}$$

Answer: The retail price of a decorative pillow is $\boxed{}$.

Example 2 *Finding a Sale Price*

Backpack You buy a backpack that is on sale for 25% off the original price of $20. What is the sale price?

Solution

Method 1 Subtract the discount from the original price.

Sale price = Original price − Discount

= ☐ − ☐ · ☐ Substitute.

= ☐ − ☐ · ☐ Write ☐ as a decimal.

= ☐ − ☐ Multiply.

= ☐ Subtract.

Method 2 Multiply the original price by (100% − Discount percent).

Sale price = Original price · (100% − Discount percent)

= ☐ · (100% − ☐) Substitute.

= ☐ · ☐ Subtract percents.

= ☐ · ☐ Write ☐ as a decimal.

= ☐ Multiply.

Answer: The sale price of the backpack is $☐.

✔ **Checkpoint**

1. In Example 1, what is the retail price of a decorative pillow if the markup percent is 250%?

2. A pair of shorts that originally costs $15 is 40% off. Find the sale price.

Example 3   *Using Sales Tax and Tips*

Pizza You order pizza to be delivered. The bill is $18. You give the delivery person a 15% tip. The sales tax is 5%. What is the total cost of the pizza?

Solution

Sales tax and tips are calculated using a percent of the purchasing price. These amounts are then added to the purchase price.

Total = Food bill + Sales tax + Tip

$$= \boxed{} + \boxed{} \cdot \boxed{} + \boxed{} \cdot \boxed{} \qquad \text{Substitute.}$$

$$= \boxed{} + \boxed{} \cdot \boxed{} + \boxed{} \cdot \boxed{} \qquad \begin{array}{l}\text{Write percents}\\\text{as decimals.}\end{array}$$

$$= \boxed{} \qquad \text{Evaluate.}$$

Answer: The total cost of the pizza is $ \boxed{} .

✔ Checkpoint

3. In Example 3, find the total cost of the pizza if the tip is 20%.

Example 4   *Finding an Original Amount*

Blender A store marks up the wholesale price of a blender by 125%. The retail price is $30. What is the wholesale price?

Solution

Let *x* represent the wholesale price.

Retail price = Wholesale price · (100% + Markup percent)

$$\boxed{} = x \cdot \left(100\% + \boxed{}\right) \qquad \text{Substitute.}$$

$$\boxed{} = x \cdot \boxed{} \qquad \text{Add percents.}$$

$$\boxed{} = x \cdot \boxed{} \qquad \text{Write } \boxed{} \text{ as a decimal.}$$

$$\boxed{} \approx x \qquad \text{Divide each side by } \boxed{} .$$

Answer: The wholesale price of the blender is about $ \boxed{} .

7.7 Simple and Compound Interest

Goal: Calculate interest earned and account balances.

Vocabulary

Interest:

Principal:

Simple interest:

Annual interest rate:

Balance:

Compound interest:

Simple Interest Formula

Simple interest I is given by the formula

$I = Prt$

where P is the principal, r is the annual interest rate (written as a decimal), and t is the time in years.

Example 1   *Finding Simple Interest*

A $2000 bond earns 3% simple interest per year on its purchase price. Find the interest earned after 5 years.

Solution

$I = Prt$ Write simple interest formula.

$= \boxed{}$ Substitute.

$= \boxed{}$ Multiply.

Answer: The bond will earn $ \boxed{} in interest after 5 years.

Example 2   *Finding an Interest Rate*

You deposit $900 into an account that earns simple annual interest. After 8 months, the balance is $913.20. Find the annual interest rate.

Solution

Because t in the formula $A = P(1 + rt)$ is the time in years, write 8 months as $\dfrac{8}{12}$, or $\dfrac{2}{3}$ year. Then solve for r after substituting values for A, P, and t in $A = P(1 + rt)$.

$A = P(1 + rt)$ Write formula for finding balance.

$\boxed{} = \boxed{}\left[1 + r\boxed{} \right]$ Substitute.

$\boxed{} = \boxed{} + \boxed{}\, r$ Distributive property

$\boxed{} = \boxed{}\, r$ Subtract $\boxed{}$ from each side.

$\boxed{} = r$ Divide each side by $\boxed{}$.

Answer: The annual interest rate is $\boxed{}$ %.

✓ **Checkpoint**

1. A $1200 bond earns 5% simple interest per year on its purchase price. Find the interest earned after 3 years.

Find the unknown quantity for an account that earns simple annual interest.

2. $A = \underline{\ ?\ }$, $P = \$1300$, $r = 4\%$, $t = 4$ years	3. $A = \$1116.50$, $P = \$1100$, $r = 3\%$, $t = \underline{\ ?\ }$

Compound Interest Formula

When an account earns interest compounded annually, the balance A is given by the formula

$$A = P(1 + r)^t$$

where P is the principal, r is the annual interest rate (written as a decimal), and t is the time in years.

Example 3 *Calculating Compound Interest*

You deposit $1250 into an account that earns 2.25% interest compounded annually. Find the balance after 4 years.

Solution

$A = P(1 + r)^t$ Write formula.

$= \boxed{}\left(1 + \boxed{}\right)^{\boxed{}}$ Substitute.

$\approx \boxed{}$ Use a calculator.

Answer: The balance of the account after 4 years is about $\boxed{}$.

7 Words to Review

Give an example of the vocabulary word.

Percent

Percent of change

Percent of increase

Percent of decrease

Markup

Discount

Interest

Principal

Simple interest

Annual interest rate

Balance

Compound interest rate

Review your notes and Chapter 7 by using the Chapter Review on pages 368–371 of your textbook.

8.1 Relations and Functions

Goal: Use graphs to represent relations and functions.

Vocabulary

Relation:

Domain:

Range:

Input:

Output:

Function:

Vertical
line test:

Example 1 *Identifying the Domain and Range*

Identify the domain and range of the relation represented by
the table below that shows one Norway Spruce tree's height
at different ages.

Age (years), x	5	10	15	20	25
Height (ft), y	13	25	34	43	52

Solution

The relation consists of the ordered pairs

. The domain of the relation is the set of all

, or   . The range is the set of all   ,

or   .

Domain: Range:

Example 2   *Representing a Relation*

Represent the relation (−3, 2), (−2, −2), (1, 1), (1, 3), (2, −3) as indicated.

a. A graph   **b.** A mapping diagram

Solution

a. Graph the ordered pairs as [＿＿＿＿] in a coordinate plane.

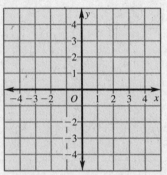

b. List the inputs and the outputs in order. Draw arrows from the [＿＿＿＿] to their [＿＿＿＿].

Input	Output

Example 3   *Identifying Functions*

Tell whether the relation is a function.

a. The relation in Example 1.

b. The relation in Example 2.

Solution

a. The relation [＿＿＿] a function because [＿＿＿＿＿＿＿＿＿] [＿＿＿＿＿＿＿＿＿]. This makes sense, as a single tree can have [＿＿＿＿＿] height at a given point in time.

b. The relation [＿＿＿] a function because [＿＿＿＿＿＿] [＿＿＿＿＿＿＿＿＿].

✔ **Checkpoint** Identify the domain and range of the relation and tell whether the relation is a function.

1. $(-5, 2), (-3, -1), (-1, 0),$ $(2, 3), (5, 4)$	**2.** $(-4, -3), (-3, 2), (0, 0),$ $(1, -1), (2, 3), (3, 1), (3, -2)$

Example 4 *Using the Vertical Line Test*

> To understand why the vertical line test works, remember that a function has exactly one output for each input.

a. In the graph below, no vertical line passes through more than one point. So, the relation represented by the graph

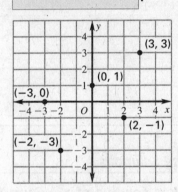

b. In the graph below, the vertical line shown passes through two points. So, the relation represented by the graph

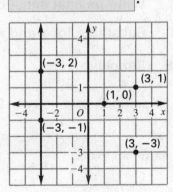

Linear Equations in Two Variables

Goal: Find solutions of equations in two variables.

Vocabulary

Equation in
two variables:

Solution of an
equation in
two variables:

Graph of an
equation in
two variables:

Linear
equation:

Function form:

Example 1 *Checking Solutions*

Tell whether $(5, -1)$ is a solution of $x - 3y = 8$.

Solution

$$x - 3y = 8 \qquad \text{Write original equation.}$$

$$\boxed{} - 3\left(\boxed{}\right) \stackrel{?}{=} 8 \qquad \text{Substitute for } x \text{ and for } y.$$

$$\boxed{}\boxed{}\, 8 \qquad \text{Simplify.}$$

Answer: $(5, -1)$ $\boxed{}$ a solution of $x - 3y = 8$.

✓ *Checkpoint* **Tell whether the ordered pair is a solution of**
2x − y = 5.

1. (0, −5)	**2.** (3, 2)	**3.** (−2, −9)

Example 2 *Graphing a Linear Equation*

Graph y = −x + 1.

1. Make a table of solutions.

x	−2	−1	0	1	2
y					

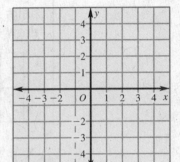

2. List the solutions as ordered pairs.

$\left(-2,\boxed{}\right), \left(-1,\boxed{}\right), \left(0,\boxed{}\right),$

$\left(1,\boxed{}\right), \left(2,\boxed{}\right)$

3. Graph the ordered pairs, and note that the points lie on a
⬜. Draw the ⬜, which is the graph of y = −x + 1.

Example 3 *Graphing Horizontal and Vertical Lines*

Graph y = −2 and x = 3.

a. The graph of the equation
y = −2 is ⬜
⬜.

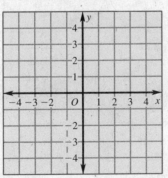

b. The graph of the equation
x = 3 is ⬜
⬜.

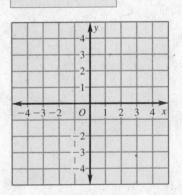

Example 4 *Writing an Equation in Function Form*

Write 3x − y = 2 in function form. Then graph the equation.

To write the equation in function form, solve for ☐.

$3x - y = 2$ Write original equation.

☐ = ☐ + 2 Subtract ☐ from each side.

☐ = ☐ − 2 Multiply each side by ☐.

To graph the equation, use its function form to make a table of solutions. Graph the ordered pairs (x, y) from the table, and draw a line through the points.

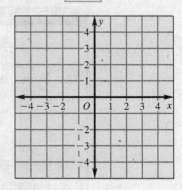

x	−1	0	1	2
y				

✔ *Checkpoint*

4. Graph y = 4 and x = −3. Tell whether each equation is a function.

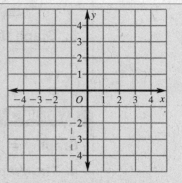

5. Write x − 2y = 4 in function form. Then graph the equation.

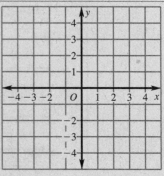

8.3 Using Intercepts

Goal: Use *x*- and *y*-intercepts to graph linear equations.

Vocabulary

x-intercept: _____

y-intercept: _____

Finding Intercepts

To find the *x*-intercept of a line, substitute ☐ for *y* in the line's equation and solve for ☐ .

To find the *y*-intercept of a line, substitute ☐ for *x* in the line's equation and solve for ☐ .

Example 1 *Finding Intercepts of a Graph*

Find the intercepts of the graph of $2x - 5y = -10$.

To find the *x*-intercept, let $y = $ ☐ and solve for *x*.

$$2x - 5y = -10 \qquad \text{Write original equation.}$$

$$2x - 5(\boxed{}) = -10 \qquad \text{Substitute for } y.$$

$$\boxed{} = -10 \qquad \text{Simplify.}$$

$$x = \boxed{} \qquad \text{Divide each side by } \boxed{}.$$

To find the *y*-intercept, let *x* = ☐ and solve for *y*.

$$2x - 5y = -10$$ Write original equation.

$$2(\boxed{}) - 5y = -10$$ Substitute for *x*.

$$\boxed{} = -10$$ Simplify.

$$y = \boxed{}$$ Divide each side by ☐.

The intercepts of a graph are numbers, not ordered pairs.

Answer: The *x*-intercept is ☐, and the *y*-intercept is ☐.

Example 2 Using Intercepts to Graph a Linear Equation

Graph the equation $2x - 5y = -10$ from Example 1.

The *x*-intercept is ☐, so plot the point $(\boxed{}, 0)$. The *y*-intercept is ☐, so plot the point $(0, \boxed{})$.

Draw a line through the two points.

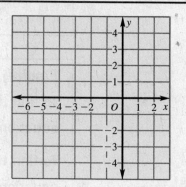

✔ **Checkpoint** Find the intercepts of the equation's graph. Then graph the equation.

1. $2x + 3y = 6$

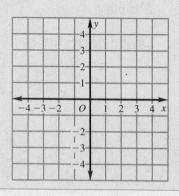

2. $3x - 6y = 12$

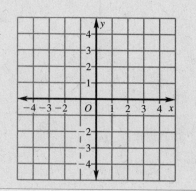

Example 3 — Writing and Graphing an Equation

Fitness You run and walk on a fitness trail that is 12 miles long. You can run 6 miles per hour and walk 3 miles per hour. Write and graph an equation describing your possible running and walking times on the fitness trail. Give three possible combinations of running and walking times.

Solution

1. To write an equation, let *x* be the running time and let *y* be the walking time (both in hours). First write a verbal model.

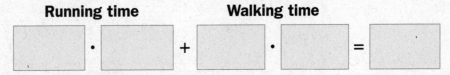

Running time   **Walking time**

☐ · ☐ + ☐ · ☐ = ☐

Then use the verbal model to write the equation.

☐

2. To graph the equation, find and use the intercepts.

Find *x*-intercept: ☐
☐
☐
☐

Find *y*-intercept: ☐
☐
☐
☐

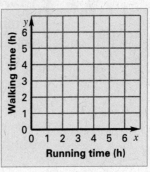

3. Three points on the graph are ☐ . So, you

can ☐

☐ .

8.4 The Slope of a Line

Goal: Find and interpret slopes of lines.

Vocabulary

Slope:

Rise:

Run:

Example 1 *Finding Slope*

A building's access ramp has a rise of 2 feet and a run of 24 feet. Find its slope.

$$\text{slope} = \frac{\text{rise}}{\boxed{}} = \boxed{} = \boxed{}$$

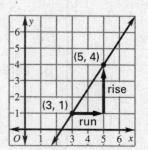
rise = 2 ft
run = 24 ft

Answer: The access ramp has a slope of $\boxed{}$.

Slope of a Line

Given two points on a nonvertical line, you can find the slope m of the line using this formula.

$$m = \frac{\text{rise}}{\text{run}}$$

$$= \frac{\text{difference of } y\text{-coordinates}}{\text{difference of } x\text{-coordinates}}$$

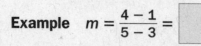
(5, 4)
rise
(3, 1)
run

Example $\quad m = \dfrac{4-1}{5-3} = \boxed{}$

Example 2 *Finding Positive and Negative Slope*

Find the slope of the line shown.

a. $m = \dfrac{\text{rise}}{\text{run}}$

$= \dfrac{\text{difference of } y\text{-coordinates}}{\text{difference of } x\text{-coordinates}}$

> When you calculate a slope, be sure to use the *x*- and *y*-coordinates of the two points in the same order.

$=$ [ ]

$=$ [ ]

Answer: The slope is [ ].

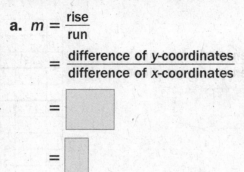

b. $m = \dfrac{\text{rise}}{\text{run}}$

$= \dfrac{\text{difference of } y\text{-coordinates}}{\text{difference of } x\text{-coordinates}}$

$=$ [ ]

$=$ [ ] $=$ [ ]

Answer: The slope is [ ].

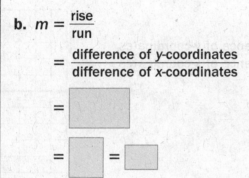

✔ *Checkpoint* **Find the slope of the line through the given points.**

1. (2, −2), (0, 4)	**2.** (7, 5), (3, 2)	**3.** (−2, 4), (6, 2)

Example 3 *Zero and Undefined Slope*

Find the slope of the line shown.

a. $m = \dfrac{\text{rise}}{\text{run}}$

$\quad = \dfrac{\text{difference of } y\text{-coordinates}}{\text{difference of } x\text{-coordinates}}$

$\quad = \boxed{}$

$\quad = \boxed{} = \boxed{}$

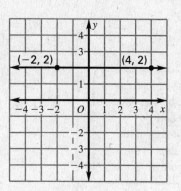

Answer: The slope is $\boxed{}$.

b. $m = \dfrac{\text{rise}}{\text{run}}$

$\quad = \dfrac{\text{difference of } y\text{-coordinates}}{\text{difference of } x\text{-coordinates}}$

$\quad = \boxed{}$

$\quad = \boxed{}$

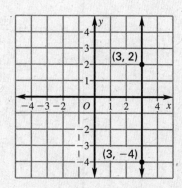

Answer: The slope is $\boxed{}$.

✔ *Checkpoint* **Find the slope of the line through the given points. Tell whether the slope is *positive*, *negative*, *zero*, or *undefined*.**

4. $(3, -1), (3, 5)$	**5.** $(-2, 5), (3, 4)$	**6.** $(1, -1), (7, -1)$

8.5 Slope-Intercept Form

Goal: Graph linear equations in slope-intercept form.

Slope-Intercept Form

Words A linear equation of the form $y = mx + b$ is said to be in slope-intercept form. The ⬚ is m and the ⬚ is b.

Algebra $y = mx + b$ **Numbers** $y = 2x + 3$

Example 1   *Identifying the Slope and y-Intercept*

Identify the slope and y-intercept of the line.

a. $y = 2x - 3$ **b.** $4x + 3y = 9$

Solution

a. Write the equation $y = 2x - 3$ as ⬚ .

   Answer: The line has a slope of ⬚ and a y-intercept of ⬚ .

b. Write the equation $4x + 3y = 9$ in slope-intercept form.

   $4x + 3y = 9$ Write original equation.

   $3y = $ ⬚   Subtract ⬚ from each side.

   $y = $ ⬚   Multiply each side by ⬚ .

   Answer: The line has a slope of ⬚ and a y-intercept of ⬚ .

✔ **Checkpoint**   Identify the slope and y-intercept of the line with the given equation.

1. $y = -3x - 4$	**2.** $x - 2y = 10$

Example 2 *Graphing an Equation in Slope-Intercept Form*

Graph the equation $y = -\frac{3}{4}x + 2$.

1. The *y*-intercept is ⬚ , so plot the point ⬚ .

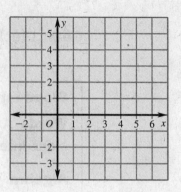

2. The slope is ⬚ = $\dfrac{-⬚}{⬚}$

   Starting at ⬚ , plot another point by moving right ⬚ units and down ⬚ units.

3. Draw a line through the two points.

If *m* is any nonzero number, then the negative reciprocal of *m* is $-\frac{1}{m}$. Note that the product of a number and its negative reciprocal is -1:

$$m\left(-\frac{1}{m}\right) = -1$$

Slopes of Parallel and Perpendicular Lines

Two nonvertical parallel lines have [   ] . For example, the parallel lines *a* and *b* below [   ] .

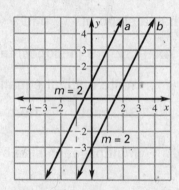

$a \parallel b$

Two nonvertical perpendicular lines, such as lines *a* and *c* below, have slopes that are [   ] .

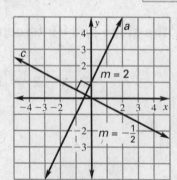

$a \perp c$

Find the slope of a line that has the given relationship to the line with the equation $5x + 2y = 10$.

a. Parallel to the line   **b.** Perpendicular to the line

Solution

a. First write the given equation in slope-intercept form.

$$5x + 2y = 10 \qquad \text{Write original equation.}$$

$$2y = \boxed{} + 10 \qquad \text{Subtract } \boxed{} \text{ from each side.}$$

$$y = \boxed{} \qquad \text{Multiply each side by } \boxed{}.$$

The slope of the given line is $\boxed{}$. Because parallel lines

have $\boxed{}$, the slope of the parallel line is

also $\boxed{}$.

b. From part (a), the slope of the given line is $\boxed{}$. So, the slope

of a line perpendicular to the given line is $\boxed{}$

$\boxed{}$ of $\boxed{}$, or $\boxed{}$.

✔ **Checkpoint**   For the line with the given equation, find the slope of a parallel line and the slope of a perpendicular line.

3. $y = -5x - 4$	**4.** $2x - 3y = 6$

8.6 Writing Linear Equations

Goal: Write linear equations.

Vocabulary

Best-fitting line:

Example 1 *Writing an Equation Given the Slope and y-Intercept*

Write an equation of the line with a slope of −2 and a
y-intercept of −5.

$y = mx + b$	Write general slope-intercept equation.
$y = \boxed{}\, x + \boxed{}$	Substitute for m and for b.
$y = \boxed{}$	Simplify.

✓ *Checkpoint*

1. Write an equation of the line with a slope of 4 and a y-intercept
   of −3.

Example 2 *Writing an Equation of a Graph*

Write an equation of the line shown.

1. Find the slope m using the labeled points.

   $m = \boxed{} = \boxed{}$

2. Find the y-intercept b. The line crosses

   the $\boxed{}$ at $\boxed{}$, so $b = \boxed{}$.

3. Write an equation of the form $y = mx + b$.

   $y = \boxed{}\, x + \boxed{}$

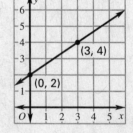

(3, 4)

(0, 2)

Example 3 *Writing Equations of Parallel or Perpendicular Lines*

a. Write an equation of the line that is parallel to the line $y = 8x$ and passes through the point $(0, 3)$.

b. Write an equation of the line that is perpendicular to the line $y = -\frac{1}{2}x + 3$ and passes through the point $(0, -5)$.

Solution

a. The slope of the given line is ☐ , so the slope of the parallel line is also ☐ . The parallel line passes through $(0, 3)$, so its y-intercept is ☐ .

Answer: An equation of the line is ☐ .

b. Because the slope of the given line is ☐ , the slope of the perpendicular line is the negative reciprocal of ☐ , or ☐ . The perpendicular line passes through $(0, 5)$, so its y-intercept is ☐ .

Answer: An equation of the line is ☐ .

✔ *Checkpoint*

2. Write an equation of the line through the points $(0, -3)$ and $(4, 5)$.

3. Write an equation of the line that is parallel to $y = 3x + 2$ and passes through the point $(0, 4)$.

4. Write an equation of the line that is perpendicular to $y = 3x + 2$ and passes through the point $(0, -2)$.

Example 4 *Approximating a Best-Fitting Line*

Teachers The table shows the number of elementary and secondary school teachers in the United States for the years 1992–1999.

Years since 1992, x	0	1	2	3	4	5	6	7
Teachers (in ten thousands), y	282	287	293	298	305	313	322	330

a. Approximate the equation of the best-fitting line for the data.

b. Predict the number of teachers in 2006.

Solution

a. *First*, make a scatter plot of the data pairs.

Next, draw the line that appears to best fit the data points. There should be about the same number of points above the line as below it. The line does not have to pass through any of the data points.

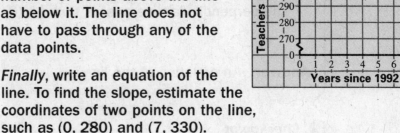

Teachers (ten thousands) — Years since 1992

Finally, write an equation of the line. To find the slope, estimate the coordinates of two points on the line, such as (0, 280) and (7, 330).

$$m = \boxed{} = \boxed{} \approx \boxed{}$$

The line intersects the y-axis at $\boxed{}$, so the y-intercept is $\boxed{}$.

Answer: An approximate equation of the best fitting line is $y = \boxed{}$.

b. Note that 2006 – 1992 = $\boxed{}$, so 2006 is $\boxed{}$ years after 1992. Calculate y when x = $\boxed{}$ using the equation from part (a).

$$y = \boxed{} \approx \boxed{}$$

Answer: In 2006, there will be about $\boxed{}$ teachers in the United States.

8.7 Function Notation

Goal: Use function notation.

Example 1   Working with Function Notation

Let $f(x) = 2x - 5$. Find $f(x)$ when $x = -3$, and find x when $f(x) = 13$.

a. $f(x) = 2x - 5$ Write function.

$f(\boxed{}) = 2(\boxed{}) - 5$ Substitute for x.

$= \boxed{}$ Simplify.

Answer: When $x = -3$, $f(x) = \boxed{}$.

b. $f(x) = 2x - 5$ Write function.

$\boxed{} = 2x - 5$ Substitute for $f(x)$.

$\boxed{} = 2x$ Add $\boxed{}$ to each side.

$\boxed{} = x$ Divide each side by $\boxed{}$.

Answer: When $f(x) = 13$, $x = \boxed{}$.

✓ *Checkpoint*   Let $g(x) = -x + 7$. Find the indicated value.

1. $g(x)$ when $x = 4$	**2.** x when $g(x) = 9$

Example 2 *Graphing a Function*

Graph the function $f(x) = \frac{5}{6}x - 3.$

1. Rewrite the function as

   [   ] .

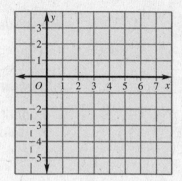

2. The *y*-intercept is [   ], so plot

   the point [   ] .

3. The slope is [   ]. Starting at

   [   ], plot another point by

   moving right [   ] units and up

   [   ] units.

4. Draw a line through the two points.

✔ **Checkpoint** **Graph the function.**

3. $g(x) = -\frac{2}{3}x + 2$

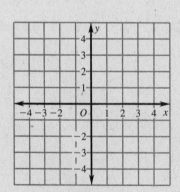

4. $h(x) = \frac{3}{2}x - 1$

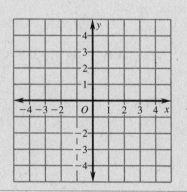

Example 3 *Writing a Function*

Write a linear function g given that g(0) = 10 and g(4) = −2.

1. Find the slope *m* of the function's graph. From the values of g(0) and g(4), you know that the graph of *g* passes through the points [ ] and [ ]. Use these points to calculate the slope.

   $$m = \boxed{} = \boxed{} = \boxed{}$$

2. Find the *y*-intercept *b* of the function's graph. The graph passes through [ ], so $b = \boxed{}$.

3. Write an equation of the form g(x) = mx + b.

   $$\boxed{}$$

Example 4 *Using Function Notation in Real Life*

You ride your bike at a speed of 12 miles per hour.

a. Use function notation to write an equation giving the distance traveled as a function of time.

b. How long will it take you to travel 30 miles?

Solution

a. Let *t* be the elapsed time (in hours) since you started riding your bike, and let d(t) be the distance traveled (in miles) at that time. Write a verbal model. Then use the verbal model to write an equation.

   $$\boxed{} = \boxed{} \cdot \boxed{}$$
   $$\boxed{} = \boxed{}$$

b. Find the value of *t* for which d(t) = 30.

   $d(t) = \boxed{}$ Write function for distance.

   $\boxed{} = \boxed{}$ Substitute for d(t).

   $\boxed{} = t$ Divide each side by $\boxed{}$.

   Answer: It will take you $\boxed{}$ hours to travel 30 miles.

Systems of Linear Equations

Goal: Graph and solve systems of linear equations.

Vocabulary

System of
linear equations:

Solution of a
linear system:

Example 1   *Solving a System of Linear Equations*

Solve the linear system: $y = x - 3$ **Equation 1**

$$y = -\frac{1}{5}x + 3$$ **Equation 2**

1. Graph the equations.

2. Identify the apparent
   intersection point, [   ].

3. Verify that [   ] is the
   solution of the system by
   substituting [   ] for x and [   ]
   for y in each equation.

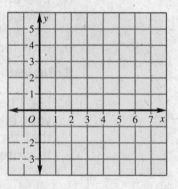

Equation 1

$$y = x - 3$$

$$\boxed{} \overset{?}{=} \boxed{} - 3$$

Equation 2

$$y = -\frac{1}{5}x + 3$$

$$\boxed{} \overset{?}{=} -\frac{1}{5}x \boxed{} + 3$$

Answer: The solution is [   ].

Example 2   *Solving a Linear System with No Solution*

Solve the linear system: $y = -3x - 2$ **Equation 1**

                        $y = -3x + 3$ **Equation 2** .

Graph the equations. The graphs appear to be [　　　] lines. You can confirm that the lines are [　　　] by observing from their equations that they have the [　　　] slope,

[　　　] , but [　　　] y-intercepts,

[　　　] and [　　　] .

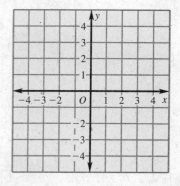

Answer: Because parallel lines [　　　　　　] , the linear system has [　　　　　] .

Example 3   *Solving a Linear System with Many Solutions*

Solve the linear system: $2x + y = 4$ **Equation 1**

                       $-6x + 3y = -12$ **Equation 2**

Write each equation in slope-intercept form and then graph the equations.

Equation 1

$2x + y = 4$

     $y =$ [　　　　]

Equation 2

$-6x - 3y = -12$

[　　　　　　　]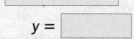

     $y =$ [　　　　]

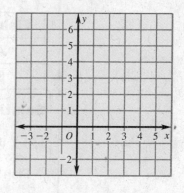

The slope-intercept forms of equations 1 and 2 are identical, so the graphs of the equations are [　　　　　　] .

Answer: Because the graphs have infinitely many [　　　　]

[　　　　　　] , the system has [　　　　　　　　] .

Any [　　] on the line [　　　　　] represents a solution.

✔ **Checkpoint** Solve the linear system by graphing.

1. $y = -x + 3$
   $y = \frac{1}{3}x - 1$

2. $5x + y = -3$
   $10x + 2y = 8$

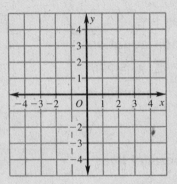

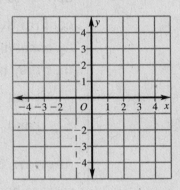

Example 4 *Writing and Solving a Linear System*

An ecologist is studying the population of two types of fish in a lake. Use the information in the table to predict when the population of the two types of fish will be the same.

Fish type	Current population	Change (number per year)
A	340	−25
B	180	15

Solution

Let y be the number of fish after x years. Write a linear system.

Fish A population:

Fish B population:

Use a graphing calculator to graph the equations. Trace along one of the graphs until the cursor is on the point of intersection. This point is   .

Answer: The number of fish will be the same after   years when the population of each fish will be   .

8.9 Graphs of Linear Inequalities

Goal: Graph inequalities in two variables.

Vocabulary

Linear
inequality:

Solution of a
linear inequality:

Graph of a
linear inequality:

Example 1   Checking Solutions of a Linear Inequality

Tell whether the ordered pair is a solution of $3x - y > 2$.

a. (3, 0)   **b.** (−1, 5)

Solution

a. Substitute for x and for y.

$$3x - y > 2$$

$$3\boxed{} - \boxed{} \overset{?}{>} 2$$

$$\boxed{}\boxed{}\boxed{}$$

(3, 0) $\boxed{}$ a solution.

b. Substitute for x and for y.

$$3x - y > 2$$

$$3\boxed{} - \boxed{} \overset{?}{>} 2$$

$$\boxed{}\boxed{}\boxed{}$$

(−1, 5) $\boxed{}$ a solution.

✓ Checkpoint **Tell whether the ordered pair is a solution of**
$-x + 2y > 4$.

1. (1, 6)	2. (−7, −2)	3. (2, 3)

Graphing Linear Inequalities

1. Find the equation of the boundary line by replacing the inequality symbol with =. Graph this equation. Use a dashed line for < or >. Use a solid line for ≤ or ≥.

2. Test a point in one of the half-planes to determine whether it is a solution of the inequality.

3. If the test point is a solution, shade the half-plane that contains the point. If not, shade the other half-plane.

Example 2 *Graphing a Linear Inequality*

Graph $y \geq -x + 1$.

1. Draw the boundary line $y = -x + 1$. The inequality symbol is ≥, so use a

   [   ] .

2. Test the point (0, 0) in the inequality.

   $y \geq -x + 1$

   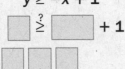 + 1

   [ ][ ][ ]

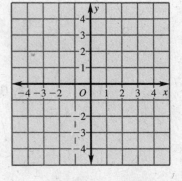

3. Because (0, 0) [   ] a solution, shade the half-plane that

   [   ] .

Example 3   *Graphing Inequalities with One Variable*

Graph x > −2 and y ≤ 3 in a coordinate plane.

a. Graph x = −2 using a line. Use (0, 0) as a test point.

$x > -2$

Shade the half-plane

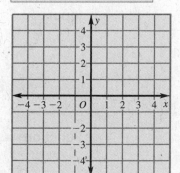

b. Graph y = 3 using a ⬚ line. Use (0, 0) as a test point.

$y \leq 3$

Shade the half-plane

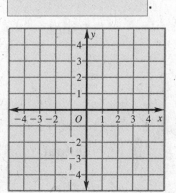

✓ **Checkpoint**   **Graph the inequality in a coordinate plane.**

4. $6x - 3y < 9$

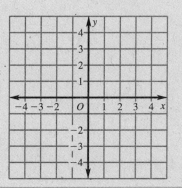

5. $x \leq 4$

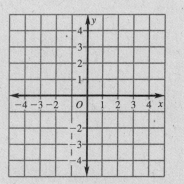

Words to Review

Give an example of the vocabulary word.

Relation

Domain

Range

Input

Output

Function

Vertical line test

Equation in two variables

Solution of an equation in two variables

Graph of an equation in two variables

Linear equation

Function form

x-intercept

y-intercept

Slope

Rise

Run

Slope-intercept form

Function notation

System of linear equations

Solution of a linear system

Linear inequality in two variables

Solution of a linear inequality in two variables

Graph of linear inequality in two variables

Review your notes and Chapter 8 by using the Chapter Review on pages 442–445 of your textbook.

Square Roots

Goal: Find and approximate square roots of numbers.

Vocabulary

Square
root:

Perfect
square:

Radical
expression:

Example 1   *Finding a Square Root*

Playground A community is building
a playground on a square plot of land
with an area of 625 square yards.
What is the length of each side of the
plot of land?

$A = 625 \text{ yd}^2$

Solution

The plot of land is a square with an area of 625 square
yards, so the length of each side of the plot of land is the

> Because length
> cannot be negative, it
> doesn't make sense
> to find the negative
> square root.

$\sqrt{625} = \boxed{}$ because $\boxed{} = 625$.

Answer: The length of each side of the plot of land is $\boxed{}$.

✓ *Checkpoint*   **Find the square roots of the number.**

1. 9	**2.** 49	**3.** 169	**4.** 196

Example 2   *Approximating a Square Root*

Approximate $\sqrt{28}$ to the nearest integer.

The perfect square closest to, but less than, 28 is ☐. The perfect square closest to, but greater than, 28 is ☐. So, 28 is between ☐ and ☐. This statement can be expressed by the *compound inequality* ☐ $< 28 <$ ☐.

☐ $< 28 <$ ☐   Identify perfect squares closest to 28.

☐ $< \sqrt{28} <$ ☐   Take positive square root of each number.

☐ $< \sqrt{28} <$ ☐   Evaluate square root of each perfect square.

Answer: Because 28 is closer to ☐ than to ☐, $\sqrt{28}$ is closer to ☐ than to ☐. So, to the nearest integer, $\sqrt{28} \approx$ ☐.

✔ *Checkpoint*   **Approximate the square root to the nearest integer.**

5. $\sqrt{46}$	6. $-\sqrt{125}$	7. $\sqrt{68.9}$	8. $-\sqrt{87.5}$

Example 3   *Using a Calculator*

Use a calculator to approximate $\sqrt{636}$. Round to the nearest tenth.

Keystrokes	Display	Answer
2nd [$\sqrt{\ }$] 636) =		

✓ Checkpoint Use a calculator to approximate the square root. Round to the nearest tenth.

9. $\sqrt{6}$	10. $-\sqrt{104}$	11. $-\sqrt{819}$	12. $\sqrt{1874}$

Example 4 *Evaluating a Radical Expression*

Evaluate $5\sqrt{a^2 - b}$ when $a = 6$ and $b = 27$.

$5\sqrt{a^2 - b} = $ ⬜   Substitute for a and for b.

$= $ ⬜   Evaluate expression inside radical symbol.

$= $ ⬜   Evaluate square root.

$= $ ⬜   Multiply.

✓ Checkpoint Evaluate the expression when $a = 16$ and $b = 9$.

13. $-\sqrt{a + b}$	14. $\sqrt{b^2 - 2a}$	15. $2\sqrt{ab}$

9.2 Simplifying Square Roots

Goal: Simplify radical expressions.

Vocabulary

Simplest form:

Product Property of Square Roots

Algebra

$\sqrt{ab} = \sqrt{a} \cdot \sqrt{b}$, where $a \geq 0$ and $b \geq 0$

Numbers

$\sqrt{9 \cdot 7} = \sqrt{9} \cdot \sqrt{7} = 3\sqrt{7}$

Example 1 *Simplifying a Radical Expression*

$\sqrt{150} = $ [ ]   Factor using greatest perfect square factor.

$= $ [ ]   Product property of square roots

$= $ [ ]   Simplify.

Example 2 *Simplifying a Variable Expression*

$\sqrt{18t^2} = $ [ ]   Factor using greatest perfect square factor.

$= $ [ ]   Product property of square roots

$= $ [ ]   Simplify.

$= $ [ ]   Commutative property

✓ **Checkpoint** Simplify the expression.

1. $\sqrt{75}$	2. $\sqrt{80}$	3. $\sqrt{24r^2}$	4. $\sqrt{56m^2}$

Quotient Property of Square Roots

Algebra

$\sqrt{\dfrac{a}{b}} = \dfrac{\sqrt{a}}{\sqrt{b}}$, where $a \geq 0$ and $b > 0$

Numbers

$\sqrt{\dfrac{11}{4}} = \dfrac{\sqrt{11}}{\sqrt{4}} = \dfrac{\sqrt{11}}{2}$

Example 3 *Simplifying a Radical Expression*

$\sqrt{\dfrac{17}{25}} = $ ☐ Quotient property of square roots

$= $ ☐ Simplify.

✓ **Checkpoint** Simplify the expression.

5. $\sqrt{\dfrac{5}{9}}$	6. $\sqrt{\dfrac{21}{64}}$	7. $\sqrt{\dfrac{16z}{49}}$	8. $\sqrt{\dfrac{32y^2}{81}}$

Example 4 *Using Radical Expressions*

The expression $\sqrt{\dfrac{h}{16}}$ gives the time (in seconds) it takes an object to fall h feet.

a. Write the expression in simplest form.

b. Find the length of time it takes for an object to fall 120 feet. Give your answer to the nearest tenth of a second.

Solution

a. $\sqrt{\dfrac{h}{16}} = $ [ ]   Quotient property of square roots

$= $ [ ]   Simplify.

Answer: In simplest form, $\sqrt{\dfrac{h}{16}} = $ [ ].

b. $\dfrac{\sqrt{h}}{\boxed{}} = $ [ ]   Substitute 120 for h.

$\approx$ [ ]   Approximate using a calculator.

Answer: The length of time it takes for an object to fall 120 feet is about [ ].

✓ **Checkpoint**

9. Find the length of time it takes for an object to fall 155 feet. Give your answer to the nearest tenth of a second.

Example 3 *Identifying Right Triangles*

Determine whether the triangle with the given side lengths is a right triangle.

a. $a = 8, b = 9, c = 12$

b. $a = 7, b = 24, c = 25$

Solution

a. $a^2 + b^2 = c^2$

$\boxed{}^2 + \boxed{}^2 \overset{?}{=} \boxed{}^2$

$\boxed{} + \boxed{} \overset{?}{=} \boxed{}$

$\boxed{}\ \boxed{}\ \boxed{}$

Answer: $\boxed{}$

b. $a^2 + b^2 = c^2$

$\boxed{}^2 + \boxed{}^2 \overset{?}{=} \boxed{}^2$

$\boxed{} + \boxed{} \overset{?}{=} \boxed{}$

$\boxed{}\ \boxed{}\ \boxed{}$

Answer: $\boxed{}$

✓ *Checkpoint* Determine whether the triangle with the given side lengths is a right triangle.

4. $a = 12, b = 9, c = 15$	5. $a = 10, b = 25, c = 27$

9.4 Real Numbers

Goal: Compare and order real numbers.

Vocabulary

Irrational number:

Real numbers:

Example 1 Classifying Real Numbers

Number	Decimal Form	Decimal Type	Type
a. $\frac{7}{10}$	$\frac{7}{10} = $		
b. $\frac{2}{9}$	$\frac{2}{9} = $ ____ $= $ ____		
c. $\sqrt{5}$	$\sqrt{5} = $		

> The square root of any whole number that is not a perfect square is irrational.

Example 2 Comparing Real Numbers

Copy and complete $\sqrt{3}$ _?_ $\frac{6}{5}$ using <, >, or =.

Solution

Graph $\sqrt{3}$ and $\frac{6}{5}$ on a number line.

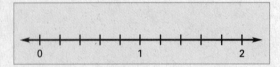

$\sqrt{3}$ is to the ____ of $\frac{6}{5}$.

Answer: $\sqrt{3}$ ☐ $\frac{6}{5}$

Example 3 *Ordering Real Numbers*

Use a number line to order the numbers $\frac{\sqrt{6}}{2}$, -2.2, $\frac{5}{2}$, and $-2\sqrt{2}$ from least to greatest.

Graph the numbers on a number line and read them from left to right.

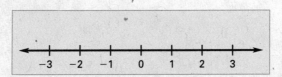

Answer: From least to greatest, the numbers are

☑ **Checkpoint** Tell whether the number is *rational* or *irrational*.

1. $\frac{8}{11}$	2. $\sqrt{7}$	3. $\sqrt{49}$	4. $\sqrt{\frac{2}{5}}$

Copy and complete the statement using <, >, or =.

5. $-\frac{3}{2}$? $-\sqrt{3}$	6. $\sqrt{10}$? 3.5

Checkpoint Use a number line to order the numbers from least to greatest.

7. $5.9, 3\sqrt{5}, \dfrac{27}{5}, \sqrt{35}$

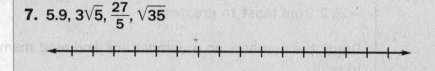

8. $-\sqrt{21}, -4.6, -\dfrac{9}{2}, -2\sqrt{5}$

Example 4 *Using Irrational Numbers*

Speed After an accident, a police officer finds that the length of a car's skid marks is 98 feet. The car's speed s (in miles per hour) and the length ℓ (in feet) of the skid marks are related by $s = \sqrt{27\ell}$. Find the car's speed to the nearest tenth of a mile per hour.

Solution

$s = \sqrt{27\ell}$ Write formula.

$= \sqrt{27 \cdot \boxed{}}$ Substitute value.

$= \sqrt{\boxed{}}$ Multiply.

$\approx \boxed{}$ Approximate using a calculator.

Answer: The car's speed was about $\boxed{}$ miles per hour.

Distance and Midpoint Formulas

Goal: Use the distance, midpoint, and slope formulas.

The Distance Formula

Words The distance between two points in a coordinate plane is equal to the square root of the sum of the horizontal change squared and the vertical change squared.

Algebra $d = \sqrt{(x_2 - x_1)^2 + (y_2 - y_1)^2}$

Example 1 *Finding the Distance Between Two Points*

Find the distance between the points $M(2, 3)$ and $N(1, 5)$.

$d = \sqrt{(x_2 - x_1)^2 + (y_2 - y_1)^2}$　　　Distance formula

$= \sqrt{\left(1 - \boxed{}\right)^2 + \left(5 - \boxed{}\right)^2}$　　　Substitute.

$= \sqrt{\left(\boxed{}\right)^2 + \boxed{}^2}$　　　Subtract.

$= \sqrt{\boxed{} + \boxed{}}$　　　Evaluate powers.

$= \boxed{}$　　　Add.

Answer: The distance between the points is $\boxed{}$ units.

✔ *Checkpoint* **Find the distance between the points. Write your answer in simplest form.**

1. $(2, -5), (-3, 7)$	**2.** $(2, -2), (0, 4)$

The Midpoint Formula

Words The coordinates of the midpoint of a segment are the average of the endpoints' x-coordinates and the average of the endpoints' y-coordinates.

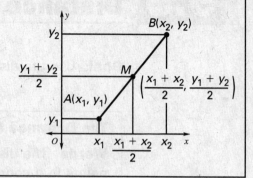

Algebra $M = \left(\dfrac{x_1 + x_2}{2}, \dfrac{y_1 + y_2}{2}\right)$

Example 2 Finding a Midpoint

Find the midpoint M of the segment with endpoints (2, 5) and (−6, −3).

$M = \left(\dfrac{x_1 + x_2}{2}, \dfrac{y_1 + y_2}{2}\right)$ Midpoint formula

$= \left(\dfrac{\boxed{} + \boxed{}}{2}, \dfrac{\boxed{} + \boxed{}}{2}\right)$ Substitute values.

$= \boxed{}$ Simplify.

✓ **Checkpoint**   Find the midpoint of the segment with the given endpoints.

3. (2, −5), (−3, 7)	4. (3, −4), (7, 2)

Slope

If points $A(x_1, y_1)$ and $B(x_2, y_2)$ do not lie on a vertical line, you can use coordinate notation to write a formula for the slope of the line through A and B.

$$\text{slope} = \frac{\text{difference of } y\text{-coordinates}}{\text{difference of } x\text{-coordinates}} = \frac{y_2 - y_1}{x_2 - x_1}$$

Example 3   *Finding Slope*

Find the slope of the line through $(2, -1)$ and $(-1, 2)$.

$\text{slope} = \dfrac{y_2 - y_1}{x_2 - x_1}$ Slope formula

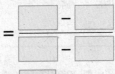   Substitute values.

   Simplify.

✓ **Checkpoint**   **Find the slope of the line through the given points.**

5. $(2, -6), (-3, 9)$	**6.** $(6, -2), (-4, 7)$

9.6 Special Right Triangles

Goal: Use special right triangles to solve problems.

45°-45°-90° Triangle

Words In a 45°-45°-90° triangle, the length of the hypotenuse is the product of the length of a leg and $\sqrt{2}$.

Algebra hypotenuse = leg · $\sqrt{2}$

$= a\sqrt{2}$

Example 1   Using a 45°-45°-90° Triangle

A 45°-45°-90° triangle used in mechanical drawing has 10-inch legs. Find the length of the hypotenuse to the nearest tenth of an inch.

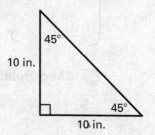

Solution

hypotenuse = leg · $\sqrt{2}$ Rule for 45°-45°-90° triangle

$=$ ☐ · $\sqrt{2}$ Substitute.

$\approx$ ☐   Use a calculator.

Answer: The length of the triangle's hypotenuse is about ☐ inches.

✔ **Checkpoint**

1. Find the unknown length *x*. Write your answer in simplest form.

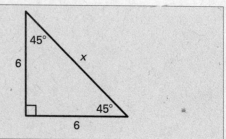

<table>
<tr><td colspan="2">

30°-60°-90° Triangle

</td></tr>
<tr><td>

In a 30°-60°-90° triangle, the shorter leg is opposite the 30° angle, and the longer leg is opposite the 60° angle.

</td><td>

Words In a 30°-60°-90° triangle, the length of the hypotenuse is twice the length of the shorter leg. The length of the longer leg is the product of the length of the shorter leg and $\sqrt{3}$.

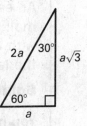

</td></tr>
</table>

Algebra hypotenuse = 2 · shorter leg = $2a$

longer leg = shorter leg · $\sqrt{3}$ = $a\sqrt{3}$

Example 2 *Using a 30°-60°-90° Triangle*

Find the length x of the hypotenuse and the length y of the longer leg of the triangle.

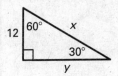

The triangle is a 30°-60°-90° triangle.
The length of the shorter leg is ☐ units.

a. hypotenuse = 2 · shorter leg

$x = 2 \cdot$ ☐

$=$ ☐

Answer: The length x of the hypotenuse is ☐ units.

b. longer leg = shorter leg · $\sqrt{3}$

$y =$ ☐ $\sqrt{3}$

Answer: The length y of the longer leg is ☐ $\sqrt{3}$ units.

✔ *Checkpoint*

2. **Find the unknown lengths x and y. Write your answers in simplest form.**

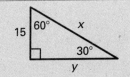

Example 3 *Using a Special Right Triangle*

An escalator going up to the second floor in a mall is 224 feet long and makes a 30° angle with the first floor. Find, to the nearest foot, the lengths of the triangle's legs.

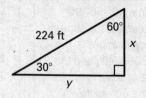

Solution

You need to find the length of the shorter leg first.

1. Find the length x of the shorter leg.

hypotenuse = 2 · shorter leg	Rule for 30°-60°-90° triangle
$\boxed{}$ = 2x	Substitute.
$\boxed{}$ = x	Divide each side by $\boxed{}$.

2. Find the length y of the longer leg.

longer leg = shorter leg · $\sqrt{3}$	Rule for 30°-60°-90° triangle
$y = \boxed{}\sqrt{3}$	Substitute.
$y \approx \boxed{}$	Use a calculator.

Answer: The length of the shorter leg is $\boxed{}$ feet and the length of the longer leg is about $\boxed{}$ feet.

9.7 The Tangent Ratio

Goal: Use tangent to find side lengths of right triangles.

Vocabulary

Trigonometric ratio:

The Tangent Ratio

The **tangent** of an acute angle of a right triangle is the ratio of the length of the side opposite the angle to the length of the side adjacent to the angle.

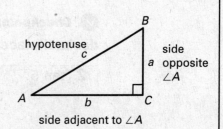

$$\tan A = \frac{\text{side opposite } \angle A}{\text{side adjacent to } \angle A} = \frac{a}{b}$$

Example 1   Finding a Tangent Ratio

For $\triangle PQR$, find the tangent of $\angle P$.

$$\tan P = \frac{\text{opposite}}{\text{adjacent}} = \boxed{}$$

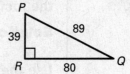

✔ **Checkpoint**

1. For $\triangle PQR$ in Example 1, find the tangent of $\angle Q$.

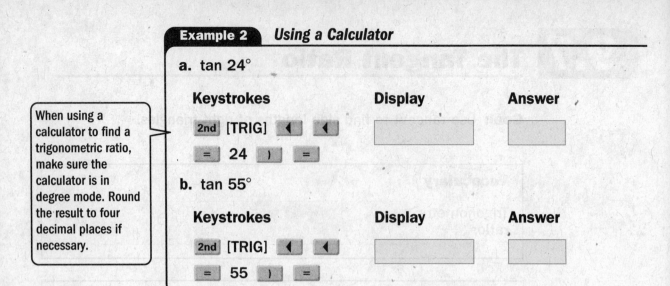

Example 2　Using a Calculator

a. tan 24°

Keystrokes	Display	Answer
2nd [TRIG] ◀ ◀		
= 24) =		

When using a calculator to find a trigonometric ratio, make sure the calculator is in degree mode. Round the result to four decimal places if necessary.

b. tan 55°

Keystrokes	Display	Answer
2nd [TRIG] ◀ ◀		
= 55) =		

✓ **Checkpoint**　Approximate the tangent value to four decimal places.

2. tan 5°	3. tan 38°	4. tan 72°

Example 3　Using a Tangent Ratio

Find the height h (in feet) of the roof to the nearest foot.

Solution

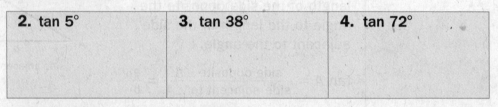

Use the tangent ratio. In the diagram, the length of the leg opposite the 27° angle is h. The length of the adjacent leg is 30 feet.

$\tan 27° = \dfrac{\text{opposite}}{\text{adjacent}}$ 　Definition of tangent ratio

$\tan 27° = \boxed{}$ 　Substitute.

$\boxed{} \approx \boxed{}$ 　Use a calculator to approximate tan 27°.

$\boxed{} \approx h$ 　Multiply each side by $\boxed{}$.

Answer: The height of the roof is about $\boxed{}$ feet.

9.8 The Sine and Cosine Ratios

Goal: Use sine and cosine to find triangle side lengths.

The Sine and Cosine Ratios

The **sine** of an acute angle of a right triangle is the ratio of the length of the side opposite the angle to the length of the hypotenuse.

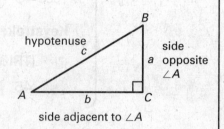

$$\sin A = \frac{\text{side opposite } \angle A}{\text{hypotenuse}} = \frac{a}{c}$$

The **cosine** of an acute angle of a right triangle is the ratio of the length of the angle's adjacent side to the length of the hypotenuse.

$$\cos A = \frac{\text{side adjacent } \angle A}{\text{hypotenuse}} = \frac{b}{c}$$

Example 1   *Finding Sine and Cosine Ratios*

For $\triangle PQR$, find the sine and cosine of $\angle P$.

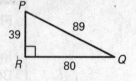

$$\sin P = \frac{\text{opposite}}{\text{hypotenuse}} = \boxed{}$$

$$\cos P = \frac{\text{adjacent}}{\text{hypotenuse}} = \boxed{}$$

✔ **Checkpoint**

1. For $\triangle PQR$ in Example 1, find the sine and cosine of $\angle Q$.

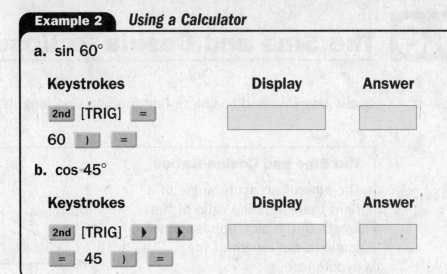

Example 2   *Using a Calculator*

a. sin 60°

Keystrokes	Display	Answer
2nd [TRIG] =		
60) =		

b. cos 45°

Keystrokes	Display	Answer
2nd [TRIG] ▶ ▶		
= 45) =		

✔ **Checkpoint**   Approximate the sine or cosine value to four
decimal places.

2. cos 9°	**3.** cos 78°	**4.** sin 13°	**5.** sin 88°

Example 3   *Using a Cosine Ratio*

Find the value of *x* in the triangle.

In △*DEF*, $\overline{DE}$ is adjacent to ∠*D*.
Because you know the length of
the hypotenuse, use cos *D* and
the definition of the cosine ratio
to find the value of *x*. Round
your answer to the nearest tenth
of a unit.

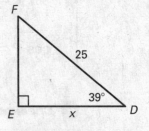

$$\cos D = \frac{\text{adjacent}}{\text{hypotenuse}}$$ Definition of cosine ratio

[   ] = [   ]   Substitute.

[   ] ≈ [   ]   Use a calculator to approximate cos 39°.

[   ] ≈ *x*   Multiply each side by [   ].

Example 4 **Using a Sine Ratio**

A ski jump is 140 meters long and makes an angle of 25° with the ground. To the nearest meter, estimate the height h of the ski jump.

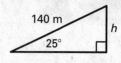

Solution

To estimate the height of the ski jump, find the length of the side [   ] the 25° angle. Because you know the length of the hypotenuse, use sin 25°.

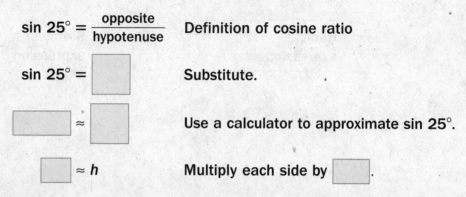

$$\sin 25° = \frac{\text{opposite}}{\text{hypotenuse}}$$ Definition of cosine ratio

$$\sin 25° = \boxed{}$$ Substitute.

$$\boxed{} \approx \boxed{}$$ Use a calculator to approximate sin 25°.

$$\boxed{} \approx h$$ Multiply each side by $\boxed{}$.

Answer: The height of the ski jump is about $\boxed{}$ meters.

9 Words to Review

Give an example of the vocabulary word.

Square root

Perfect square

Radical expression

Simplest form of a radical expression

Hypotenuse

Leg

Pythagorean theorem

Irrational number

Real number

Distance formula

Midpoint formula

Slope formula

Sine

Cosine

Tangent

Review your notes and Chapter 9 by using the Chapter Review on pages 500–503 of your textbook.

10.1 Triangles

Goal: Solve problems involving triangles.

Example 1 Classifying a Triangle by Angle Measures

In the diagram, $m\angle ABC = 44°$ and $m\angle BAC = m\angle BCA$. Find $m\angle BAC$ and $m\angle BCA$. Then classify $\triangle ABC$ by its angle measures.

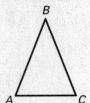

> You can classify a triangle by its angle measures or by its side lengths. When classified by angle measures, triangles are acute, right, obtuse, or equiangular. When classified by side lengths, triangles are equilateral, isosceles, or scalene.

Solution

Let $x°$ represent $m\angle BAC$ and $m\angle BCA$.

$$m\angle BAC + m\angle BCA + m\angle ABC = 180°$$ — Sum of angle measures is 180°.

$$\boxed{} + \boxed{} + \boxed{} = 180°$$ — Substitute values.

$$\boxed{} + \boxed{} = 180$$ — Combine like terms.

$$\boxed{} = \boxed{}$$ — Subtract $\boxed{}$ from each side.

$$x = \boxed{}$$ — Divide each side by $\boxed{}$.

Answer: $m\angle BAC = m\angle BCA = \boxed{}$. Because $\angle BAC$, $\angle BCA$, and $\angle ABC$ are $\boxed{}$, $\triangle ABC$ is $\boxed{}$.

✔ **Checkpoint** Find the value of x. Then classify the triangle by its angle measures.

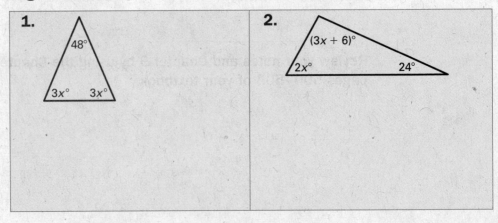

1. 48° 3x° 3x°

2. (3x + 6)° 2x° 24°

Example 2 **Finding Unknown Side Lengths**

The perimeter of a scalene triangle is 45 inches. The length of the first side is twice the length of the second side. The length of the third side is 15 inches. Find the lengths of the other two sides.

Solution

Draw the triangle. Let x and $2x$ represent the unknown side lengths. Write an equation for the perimeter P. Then solve for x.

$P = 2x + x + 15$ Formula for perimeter

$\boxed{} = 2x + x + 15$ Substitute $\boxed{}$ for P.

$\boxed{} = \boxed{}$ Combine like terms.

$\boxed{} = \boxed{}$ Subtract $\boxed{}$ from each side.

$\boxed{} = x$ Divide each side by $\boxed{}$.

Answer: The length of the second side is $\boxed{}$ inches, and the length of the first side is $2\left(\boxed{}\right) = \boxed{}$ inches.

✔ **Checkpoint** Find the unknown side length of the triangle given the perimeter P. Then classify the triangle by its side lengths.

3. $P = 75$ ft

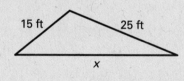

15 ft   25 ft

x

4. $P = 21.6$ m

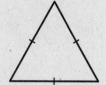

Example 3   *Finding Angle Measures Using a Ratio*

The ratio of the angle measures of a triangle is $3:4:5$. Find the angle measures. Then classify the triangle by its angle measures.

Solution.

> For a triangle whose angles measure 50°, 60°, and 70°, you can say that the ratio of the angle measures is $50:60:70$, or $5:6:7$. Therefore, if you know that the ratio of the angle measures is $5:6:7$, you can say that the angle measures are $5x°$, $6x°$, and $7x°$ for some value of x.

1. Let ⬜ , ⬜ , and ⬜ represent the angle measures. Write an equation for the sum of the angle measures.

$$\boxed{} + \boxed{} + \boxed{} = 180°$$ Sum of angle measures is 180°.

$$\boxed{} = 180$$ Combine like terms.

$$x = \boxed{}$$ Divide each side by ⬜.

2. Substitute ⬜ for x in the expression for each angle measure.

$$\left(3 \cdot \boxed{}\right)° = \boxed{} \qquad \left(4 \cdot \boxed{}\right)° = \boxed{} \qquad \left(5 \cdot \boxed{}\right)° = \boxed{}$$

Answer: The angle measures of the triangle are ⬜, ⬜, and ⬜. So, the triangle is ⬜⬜⬜.

✔ **Checkpoint**

5. The ratio of the angle measures of a triangle is $7:12:17$. Find the angle measures. Then classify the triangle by its angle measures.

10.2 Polygons and Quadrilaterals

Goal: Classify polygons and quadrilaterals.

Vocabulary	
Polygon:	
Regular polygon:	
Convex polygon:	
Concave polygon:	
Diagonal of a polygon:	

Polygons	Regular polygons	Not polygons

The name *n*-gon refers to a polygon that has *n* sides. For example, a 15-gon is a polygon that has 15 sides.

Names of Other Polygons

Polygons	Pentagon	Hexagon	Heptagon	Octagon	*n*-gon
Number of sides	5	6	7	8	*n*

Lesson 10.2   Polygons and Quadrilaterals   **203**

Example 1   *Identifying and Classifying Polygons*

Tell whether the figure is a polygon. If it is a polygon, classify it and tell whether it is *convex* or *concave*. If not, explain why.

a.

b.

Quadrilaterals	Diagram
Trapezoid A **trapezoid** is a quadrilateral with exactly 1 pair of parallel sides.	
Parallelogram A **parallelogram** is a quadrilateral with both pairs of opposite sides parallel.	
Rhombus A **rhombus** is a parallelogram with 4 congruent sides.	
Rectangle A *rectangle* is a parallelogram with 4 right angles.	
Square A *square* is a parallelogram with 4 right angles and 4 congruent sides.	

Example 2 · Classifying Quadrilaterals

Classify the quadrilateral.

a.

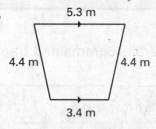

5.3 m

4.4 m   4.4 m

3.4 m

b.

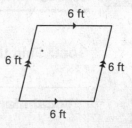

6 ft

6 ft   6 ft

6 ft

Example 3 · Finding an Unknown Angle Measure

Find the value of x.

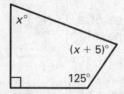

$x°$

$(x + 5)°$

$125°$

⬜ + ⬜ + ⬜ + ⬜ = 360°   Sum of angle measures in quadrilateral is 360°.

⬜ + ⬜ = 360   Combine like terms.

⬜ = ⬜   Subtract ⬜ from each side.

x = ⬜   Divide each side by ⬜.

✔ **Checkpoint** Tell whether the figure is a polygon. If it is a polygon, classify it and tell whether it is *convex* or *concave*. If not, explain why.

1.

2.

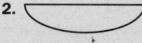

Areas of Parallelograms and Trapezoids

Goal: Find the areas of parallelograms and trapezoids.

Vocabulary

Base of a
parallelogram:

Height of a
parallelogram:

Base of a
trapezoid:

Height of
a trapezoid:

Area of a Parallelogram

Words The area A of a parallelogram is the product of the
base b and the height h.

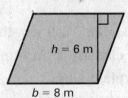

$h = 6$ m

$b = 8$ m

Algebra $A = bh$

Numbers $A = \boxed{} \cdot \boxed{} = \boxed{}$

Example 1   *Finding the Area of a Parallelogram*

The base of a parallelogram is 8 yards. The height is three times the base. Find the area of the parallelogram.

1. Find the height.

$h = 3b$

$= 3( )$

$= $

2. Find the area.

$A = bh$

$= $

$= $

Answer: The parallelogram has an area of .

Area of a Trapezoid

Words   The area A of a trapezoid is one half of the product of the sum of the bases, b_1 and b_2, and the height h.

Algebra $A = \frac{1}{2}(b_1 + b_2)h$

$b_1 = 5$ cm

$h = 4$ cm

$b_2 = 7$ cm

Numbers $A = (+) = $

Example 2   *Finding the Area of a Trapezoid*

The diagram shows one of the trapezoids in a floor design. Find the area of the trapezoid.

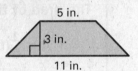

5 in.

3 in.

11 in.

Solution

$A = \frac{1}{2}(b_1 + b_2)h$ Write formula for area of a trapezoid.

$= (+) $ Substitute values.

$= $ Simplify.

Answer: The trapezoid has an area of .

✔ Checkpoint **Find the area of the parallelogram or trapezoid.**

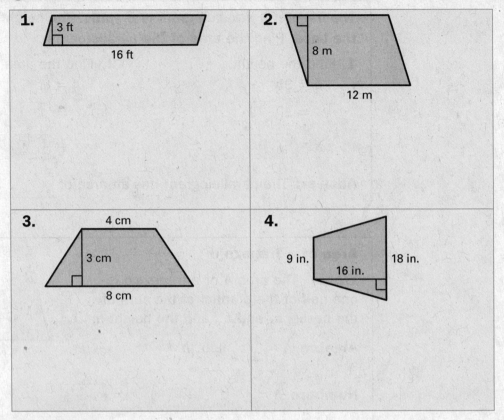

1. 3 ft
    16 ft

2. 8 m
    12 m

3. 4 cm
    3 cm
    8 cm

4. 9 in.   18 in.
    16 in.

Example 3 **Finding an Unknown Length**

The height of a trapezoid is 8 feet. One of its bases is 12 feet. The area of the trapezoid is 108 square feet. Find the other base.

$A = \frac{1}{2}(b_1 + b_2)h$ Write formula for area of a trapezoid.

$\boxed{} = \boxed{}(\boxed{} + b_2)\boxed{}$ Substitute values.

$\boxed{} = \boxed{}(\boxed{} + b_2)$ Multiply.

$\boxed{} = \boxed{} + \boxed{}$ Distributive property

$\boxed{} = \boxed{}$ Subtract ☐ from each side.

$\boxed{} = b_2$ Divide each side by ☐ .

Answer: The other base is ☐ .

Circumference and Area of a Circle

Goal: Find the circumferences and areas of circles.

Vocabulary

Circle:

Center:

Radius:

Diameter:

Circumference:

Circumference of a Circle

Words The circumference C of a circle is the product of π and the diameter d, or twice the product of π and the radius r.

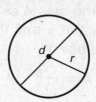

Algebra $C = \pi d$ $\qquad$ $C = 2\pi r$

Example 1   *Finding the Circumference of a Circle*

Labels A circular label has a diameter of 3.33 inches. Approximate the distance around the label to the nearest inch.

3.33 in.

Solution

$C = \pi d$

Write formula for circumference of a circle.

$\approx$ [   ] ([   ])

Substitute for π and for d.

$=$ [   ]

Multiply.

Answer: The distance around the label is about [   ].

> When the radius or diameter of a circle is divisible by 7, use $\frac{22}{7}$ to approximate π. Otherwise, use 3.14 to approximate π.

Example 2   *Finding the Radius of a Circle*

The circumference of a circle is 56 feet. Find the radius of the circle to the nearest foot.

$C = 2\pi r$

Write formula for circumference of a circle.

[   ] $\approx$ [   ] ([   ])r

Substitute for C and for π.

[   ] $\approx$ [   ] r

Multiply.

[   ] $\approx r$

Divide each side by [   ]. Use a calculator.

Answer: The radius of the circle is about [   ].

Area of a Circle

Words The area A of a circle is the product of π and the square of the radius r.

Algebra $A = \pi r^2$

Example 3 — Finding the Area of a Circle

Find the area of the circle to the nearest square meter.

1. Find the radius.

$$r = \frac{d}{2} = \frac{\boxed{}}{2} = \boxed{}$$

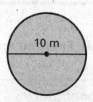

10 m

2. Find the area.

$A = \pi r^2$ Write formula for area of a circle.

$\approx \boxed{} \left(\boxed{} \right)^2$ Substitute for π and for r.

$= \boxed{}$ Simplify.

Answer: The area of the circle is about $\boxed{}$.

Example 4 — Finding the Radius of a Circle

The area of a circle is 39.25 square yards. Find the radius of the circle to the nearest tenth of a yard.

$A = \pi r^2$ Write formula for area of a circle.

$\boxed{} \approx \boxed{} r^2$ Substitute for A and for π.

$\boxed{} \approx r^2$ Divide each side by $\boxed{}$.

$\boxed{} \approx r$ Take positive square root of each side.

$\boxed{} \approx r$ Use a calculator to approximate square root.

Answer: To the nearest tenth of a yard, the radius of the circle is about $\boxed{}$.

✓ **Checkpoint** Find the circumference and the area of the circle. Round to the nearest whole number.

1.

14 cm

2.

21 ft

10.5 Surface Areas of Prisms and Cylinders

Goal: Find the surface areas of prisms and cylinders.

Vocabulary

Surface area of a solid:

Net:

> In your textbook, every prism is a *right prism*, which means that the edges connecting the bases are perpendicular to the bases.

Lateral faces of a prism:

Lateral area of a prism:

Lateral surface of a cylinder:

Lateral area of a cylinder:

Example 1   *Using a Net to Find Surface Area*

A storage chest has the shape of a rectangular prism. The net represents the storage chest. Use the net to find the surface area of the storage chest.

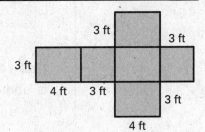

3 ft   3 ft   3 ft   4 ft   3 ft   3 ft   4 ft

1. Find the area of each face.

    Area of a rectangular face: ☐ = ☐

    Area of a square face: ☐ = ☐

2. Find the sum of the areas of the faces.

    ☐ = ☐

Answer: The surface area of the storage chest is ☐ .

Surface Area of a Prism

Words The surface area S of a prism is the sum of twice the base area B and the product of the base perimeter P and the height h.

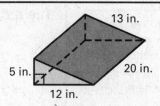

$h = 10$
$w = 4$
$\ell = 6$

Algebra $S = 2B + Ph$

Numbers $S = 2(6 \cdot 4) + [2(6) + 2(4)]10 = 148$ square units

> The formula applies to any prism. When finding the surface area of a rectangular prism, you can substitute ℓw for B and $2\ell + 2w$ for P. So, the formula becomes $S = 2\ell w + (2\ell + 2w)h$.

Example 2   *Using a Formula to Find Surface Area*

Find the surface area of the prism.

The bases of the prism are right triangles.

13 in.
5 in.
20 in.
12 in.

$S = 2B + Ph$ Write formula for surface area.

$= 2\left(\right) + \left(\right)\left(\right)$ Substitute.

$= $ Simplify.

Answer: The surface area of the prism is   .

Surface Area of a Cylinder

Words The surface area S of a cylinder is the sum of twice the base area B and the product of the base circumference C and the height h.

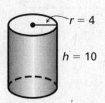

$r = 4$
$h = 10$

> In your textbook, all cylinders are *right cylinders*, which means that the segment connecting the centers of the bases is perpendicular to the bases.

Algebra $S = 2B + Ch = 2\pi r^2 + 2\pi rh$

Numbers $S = 2\pi(4)^2 + 2\pi(4)(10) \approx 352$ square units

Example 3 **Using a Formula to Find Surface Area**

Soup Can Find the surface area of the can of soup. Round your answer to the nearest tenth of an inch.

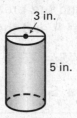

3 in.

5 in.

Solution

The radius is one half of the diameter, so $r = 1.5$ inches.

Although you used 3.14 as an approximation for π previously, you can obtain a more accurate approximation by using the π key on a calculator.

$S = 2\pi r^2 + 2\pi rh$ Write formula for surface area of a cylinder.

$= 2\pi(\boxed{})^2 + 2\pi(\boxed{})(\boxed{})$ Substitute.

$= \boxed{}\ \pi$ Simplify.

$\approx \boxed{}$ Evaluate. Use a calculator.

Answer: The surface area of the can of soup is about

$\boxed{}$.

✔ *Checkpoint* Find the surface area of the prism or cylinder. Round to the nearest whole number.

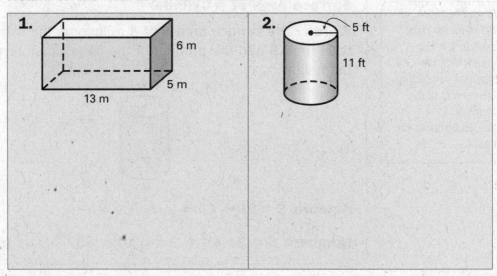

1.

6 m

5 m

13 m

2.

5 ft

11 ft

10.6 Surface Areas of Pyramids and Cones

Goal: Find the surface areas of pyramids and cones.

Vocabulary

Height of
a pyramid:

Regular
pyramid:

Slant height
of a pyramid:

Height of
a cone:

Slant height
of a cone:

Example 1   *Finding the Slant Height of a Pyramid*

> In this lesson, all pyramids are regular pyramids.

What is the slant height of the pyramid to the nearest tenth of an inch?

The slant height ℓ of the pyramid is the hypotenuse of a right triangle. The length of the legs of this triangle are 2.25 inches and 1 inch. Use the Pythagorean theorem to find the slant height.

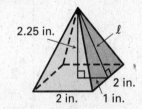

$$\boxed{}^2 + \boxed{}^2 = \ell^2 \qquad \text{Pythagorean theorem}$$

$$\boxed{} = \ell^2 \qquad \text{Simplify.}$$

$$\boxed{} \approx \ell \qquad \text{Take positive square root of each side.}$$

Answer: The slant height is about $\boxed{}$.

Surface Area of a Regular Pyramid

Words The surface area S of a regular pyramid is the sum of the base area B and one half of the product of the base perimeter P and the slant height ℓ.

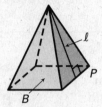

Algebra $S = B + \dfrac{1}{2}P\ell$

> This formula can be used to find the surface area of any regular pyramid.

Example 2 *Finding the Surface Area of a Regular Pyramid*

Find the surface area of the regular pyramid.

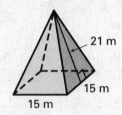

21 m

15 m

15 m

1. Find the perimeter and area of the base.

$$P = 4\left(\right) = \boxed{}$$

$$B = \boxed{}^2 = \boxed{}$$

2. Find the surface area.

$$S = B + \dfrac{1}{2}P\ell \qquad \text{Write formula for surface area of a pyramid.}$$

$$= \boxed{} + \boxed{}\left(\boxed{}\right)\left(\boxed{}\right) \qquad \text{Substitute.}$$

$$= \boxed{} \qquad \text{Simplify.}$$

Answer: The surface area of the pyramid is $\boxed{}$.

Surface Area of a Cone

Words The surface area S of a cone is the sum of the base area B and the product of π, the base radius r, and the slant height ℓ.

Algebra $S = B + \pi r \ell = \pi r^2 + \pi r \ell$

> This formula can be used to find the surface area of any cone.

Example 3 Finding the Surface Area of a Cone

Find the surface area of the cone. Round to the nearest square foot.

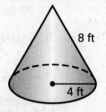

8 ft

4 ft

> In your textbook, all cones are right cones, which means that the segment connecting the center of the circular base to the vertex is perpendicular to the base.

$S = \pi r^2 + \pi r \ell$ Write formula for surface area of a cone.

$= \pi ()^2 + \pi ()()$ Substitute.

$= \boxed{} \pi \approx \boxed{}$ Simplify. Then evaluate using a calculator.

Answer: The surface area of the cone is about $\boxed{}$.

✓ **Checkpoint** Find the surface area of the pyramid or cone. Round to the nearest whole number.

1.

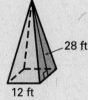

28 ft

12 ft

2.

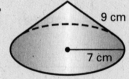

9 cm

7 cm

10.7 Volumes of Prisms and Cylinders

Goal: Find the volumes of prisms and cylinders.

Volume of a Prism

Words The volume *V* of a prism is the product of the base area *B* and the height *h*.

Algebra $V = Bh$

> This formula applies to any prism.

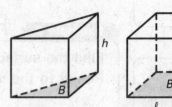

Example 1   *Finding the Volume of a Prism*

Find the volume of the prism shown.

The bases of the prism are triangles, so use the formula for the area of a triangle to find *B*.

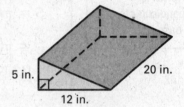

5 in.   20 in.

12 in.

$V = Bh$ Write formula for volume of a prism.

 = ( )( )( )   Substitute values.

= [   ]   Multiply.

Answer: The volume of the prism is [   ].

Volume of a Cylinder

Words The volume *V* of a cylinder is the product of the base area *B* and the height *h*.

Algebra $V = Bh = \pi r^2 h$

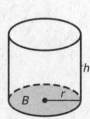

Example 2 — Finding the Volume of a Cylinder

Find the capacity (in gallons) of the recycling bin shown. Round to the nearest whole number. (Use the fact that $1 \text{ in.}^3 \approx 0.004 \text{ gal.}$)

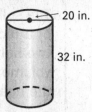

20 in.

32 in.

Solution

1. The radius is one half of the diameter. So, $r = 10$.

$V = \pi r^2 h$ — Write formula for volume of a cylinder.

$= \pi(\boxed{})^2(\boxed{})$ — Substitute values.

$= \boxed{}$ — Simplify. Leave in terms of π.

2. Use a conversion factor that converts cubic inches to gallons.

$\boxed{} \cdot \boxed{} \approx \boxed{}$ — Evaluate. Use a calculator.

Answer: The capacity of the recycling bin is about $\boxed{}$.

✓ **Checkpoint** Find the volume of the prism or cylinder. Round to the nearest whole number.

1.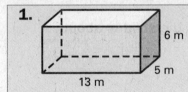

6 m
5 m
13 m

2.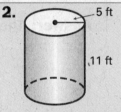

5 ft
11 ft

Example 3 *Finding the Volume of a Solid*

The solid shown is composed of a rectangular prism and two half cylinders. Find the volume of the solid. Round to the nearest cubic meter.

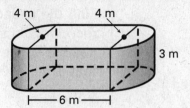

Solution

1. Find the area of a base. Each end of a base is a half circle with a radius of [ ]. Together, the ends form a complete circle.

$$B = \frac{\text{Area of}}{\text{rectangle}} + \frac{\text{Area of}}{\text{circle}}$$

$$= \ell w + \pi r^2$$ Use formulas for area of a rectangle and area of a circle.

$$= \boxed{}(\boxed{}) + \pi(\boxed{})^2$$ Substitute values.

$$= \boxed{}$$ Simplify. Leave in terms of π.

2. $V = Bh$ Write formula for volume of a prism.

$$= (\boxed{})\boxed{}$$ Substitute values.

$$= \boxed{}$$ Use distributive property.

$$\approx \boxed{}$$ Evaluate. Use a calculator.

Answer: The volume of the solid is about [ ].

10.8 Volumes of Pyramids and Cones

Goal: Find the volumes of pyramids and cones.

> ### Volume of a Pyramid or a Cone
>
> **Words** The volume V of a pyramid or a cone is one third of the product of the base area B and the height h.
>
> **Algebra** $V = \frac{1}{3}Bh$

> Unlike the formula for the surface area of a pyramid, the formula for the volume of a pyramid can also be used for pyramids whose bases are not regular.

Example 1   *Finding the Volume of a Pyramid*

Find the volume of the pyramid.

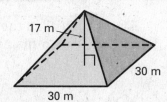

17 m

30 m

30 m

$V = \frac{1}{3}Bh$ Write formula for volume of a pyramid.

$= \frac{1}{3}\left(\boxed{}\right)\left(\boxed{}\right)$ Substitute.

$= \boxed{}$ Simplify.

Answer: The volume of the pyramid is $\boxed{}$.

✔ *Checkpoint*

1. Find the volume of the pyramid.

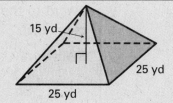

15 yd

25 yd

25 yd

Example 2 | *Finding the Volume of a Cone*

Find the volume of the cone. Round to the nearest cubic foot.

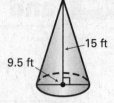

The radius is one half of the diameter, so $r =$ ◻ feet.

$V = \dfrac{1}{3}Bh$ Write formula for volume of a cone.

$\quad = \dfrac{1}{3}$◻(◻)(◻)   Substitute.

$\quad \approx$ ◻   Evaluate. Use a calculator.

Answer: The volume of the cone is about ◻.

✔ **Checkpoint**

2. Find the volume of the cone. Round to the nearest cubic centimeter.

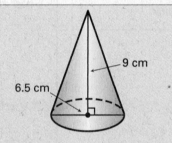

Example 3 | *Finding the Volume of a Solid*

Award The shape of an award is a pyramid. Find the volume of the award to the nearest tenth of a cubic inch.

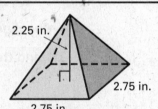

Solution

$V = \dfrac{1}{3}Bh$ Write formula for volume of a pyramid.

$\quad = \dfrac{1}{3}$(◻)(◻)   Substitute.

$\quad \approx$ ◻   Simplify.

Answer: The volume of the award is about ◻.

Give an example of the vocabulary word.

Polygon

Regular polygon

Convex polygon

Concave polygon

Diagonal of a polygon

Trapezoid

Parallelogram

Rhombus

Rectangle

Square

Base, height of a parallelogram

Bases, height of a trapezoid

Circle

Center, radius, diameter of a circle

Circumference

Surface area

Net

Lateral face of a prism

Lateral surface of a cylinder

Height, slant height of a pyramid

Regular pyramid

Height, slant height of a cone

Review your notes and Chapter 10 by using the Chapter Review on pages 564–567 of your textbook.

Stem-and-Leaf Plots and Histograms

Goal: Make stem-and-leaf plots and histograms.

Vocabulary

Stem-and-leaf plot:

Frequency:

Frequency table:

Histogram:

Example 1 · *Making a Stem-and-Leaf Plot*

The amounts (in pounds) of hay eaten by 16 elephants in one day are listed below. Use a stem-and-leaf plot to display the data.

449, 450, 419, 448, 479, 410, 446, 465,
415, 455, 479, 390, 393, 403, 460, 409

1. The least data value is ⬜ and the greatest is ⬜. Let the ⬜ be the hundreds' and tens' digits of the data values (from 39 to 47). Let the ⬜ be the ones' digits.

2. Write the stems first. Then record each amount by writing its ones' digit on the same line as its corresponding stem.

3. Make an ordered plot. Give it a key and a title.

> Each stem in a stem-and-leaf plot determines an interval. For the stem-and-leaf plot in Example 1, for instance, the stem 39 determines the interval 390-399.

Hay Eaten by Elephants

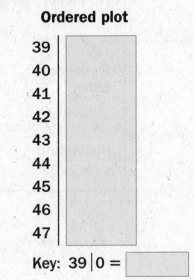

Unordered plot

| 39 |
| 40 |
| 41 |
| 42 |
| 43 |
| 44 |
| 45 |
| 46 |
| 47 |

Key: 39│0 = ⬜

Ordered plot

| 39 |
| 40 |
| 41 |
| 42 |
| 43 |
| 44 |
| 45 |
| 46 |
| 47 |

Key: 39│0 = ⬜

✔ *Checkpoint*

1. An elephant eats about 460 pounds of hay per day. How does the amount of hay this elephant eats compare to the amounts in Example 1?

Example 2 *Making a Frequency Table*

Ticket Prices The average ticket prices (rounded to the nearest dollar) charged by Major League Baseball teams in a recent year are listed below. Make a frequency table for the data.

23, 24, 20, 19, 20, 20, 19, 16, 17, 18, 17, 17, 14, 15, 14, 13, 15, 13, 12, 17, 12, 12, 12, 12, 11, 8, 10, 11, 10, 9

Solution

To choose the interval size for a frequency table, divide the range of the data by the number of intervals you want the table to have. Use the quotient as an approximate interval size.

1. Choose intervals of equal size for the data.

2. Use a tally mark to record the interval in which each data value falls.

3. Write the frequency for each interval by counting the number of tally marks for the interval.

Prices	Tally	Frequency
8–10		
11–13		
14–16		
17–19		
20–22		
23–25		

Example 3 *Making and Interpreting a Histogram*

Make a histogram using the frequency table in Example 2. Then make a conclusion about the data.

1. Show the intervals from the frequency table on the [ ] axis, and show the frequencies on the [ ] axis.

2. Draw a bar to represent the [ ] for each interval.

3. Give the histogram a title.

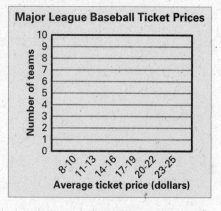

Major League Baseball Ticket Prices

Number of teams

Average ticket price (dollars)

Answer: From the histogram, about [ ] % of the teams charge $20 or more per ticket.

Box-and-Whisker Plots

Goal: Make and interpret box-and-whisker plots.

Vocabulary

Box-and-whisker plot:

Lower quartile:

Upper quartile:

Lower extreme:

Upper extreme:

Interquartile range:

Example 1   *Making a Box-and-Whisker Plot*

Store Visits A supermarket manager recorded the number of store visits for the last 7 days. The data are given below.

160, 124, 90, 130, 120, 165, 220

Display the data in a box-and-whisker plot.

Solution

First order the data to find the median, the quartiles, and the extremes.

> When a data set has an odd number of values, do not include the median in either half of the data when determining the lower and upper quartiles.

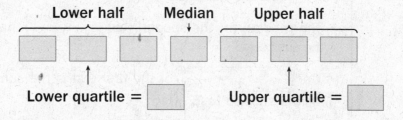

Lower quartile = ☐   Upper quartile = ☐

Plot the median, the quartiles, and the extremes below the number line.

> Plot the extremes.

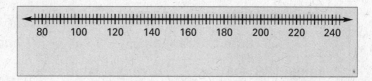

> Draw a box from the lower quartile to the upper quartile. Then draw a vertical line through the median.

> Draw a horizontal line (a "whisker") from the box to each of the extremes.

Example 2 *Comparing Box-and-Whisker Plots*

Test Scores The box-and-whisker plots below show a class's test scores for two tests. What conclusions can you make?

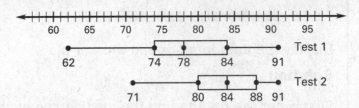

- The [   ] are the same for both tests.

- The median for the second test is [   ] than the median for the first test.

- The [   ] for the first test is the same as the [   ] for the second test.

- The scores for the [   ] are more spread out than the scores for the [   ]. Both the range $(91 - 62 = \boxed{})$ and the interquartile range $(84 - 74 = \boxed{})$ of the first test are [   ] than the range $(91 - 71 = \boxed{})$ and the interquartile range $(88 - 80 = \boxed{})$ of the second test.

✔ **Checkpoint**

1. The parking cost (in dollars) at several baseball stadiums are given below.

   6, 12, 7, 8, 6, 11, 10, 9, 15

   Make a box-and-whisker plot of the data. About what percent of the stadiums charge $9 or less?

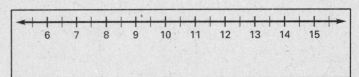

Using Data Displays

Goal: Choose appropriate displays for data sets.

Vocabulary

Categorical data:

Numerical data:

> When you choose a data display, one factor you should consider is whether the data are categorical or numerical.

Choosing Appropriate Data Displays

Use a _____ to display numerical data that change over _____ .

Use a _____ to see trends in _____ numerical data.

Use a _____ to compare categorical data.

Use a _____ to represent categorical data as parts of a _____ .

Use a _____ to organize numerical data based on their _____ .

Use a _____ to compare the _____ of numerical data that fall in equal intervals.

Use a _____ to organize numerical data into _____ of approximately equal size.

Example 1 Choosing an Appropriate Data Display

The table shows the results of a survey that asked consumers to name the day of the week they usually shop for groceries. Which display(s) can you use to display the data?

When Consumers Shop	
Day	Percent
Sunday	16%
Monday	12%
Tuesday	9%
Wednesday	13%
Thursday	12%
Friday	16%
Saturday	22%

Solution

The responses to the survey consist of the days of the week, which are [   ] data. Also, the sum of the percents is [   ]. So, you could use a [   ] to display the data. A [   ] could also be used.

✔ Checkpoint

1. The table shows the voting age population and the number who voted in 10 recent federal elections. Both numbers are given in millions. Which display(s) can you use to display the data?

Voting age population (millions)	Voter turnout (millions)
205.8	105.6
200.9	73.1
196.5	96.5
193.7	75.1
189.5	104.4
185.8	67.9
182.8	91.6
178.6	65.0
174.5	92.7
169.9	67.6

Example 2   Comparing Data Displays

Weekly Grocery Expenses An economist uses a histogram and a box-and-whisker plot to display the average weekly grocery expenses of 30 consumers. What are the advantages of each display?

a.
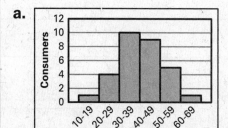

b.
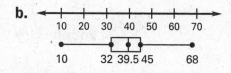

Solution

a. Using the histogram, the economist can compare the number of [   ] in each interval. For example, the economist can see that the average weekly grocery expenses for 5 of the consumers is from [   ], while the average weekly grocery expenses for [ ] of the consumers is $30 to $39.

b. Using the box-and-whisker plot, the economist can easily divide the average weekly grocery expenses into low, low-middle, high-middle, and high groups of approximately equal size. For example, the economist can conclude that about [   ] of the consumers spend $32 or less per week on groceries, and about [   ] spend from $32 to $45 per week.

Example 3   Identifying Misleading Data Displays

Electric Bill The bar graph displays a household's monthly electric bill from September to February. What is misleading about the display?

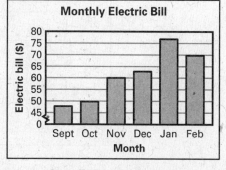

Solution

The broken vertical axis exaggerates the differences in the bar lengths. For instance, it appears that February's electric bill is [ ] times that of October's, but it is actually [ ] times larger.

Collecting Data

Goal: Identify populations and sampling methods.

Vocabulary

Population: [   ]

Sample: [   ]

Biased sample: [   ]

Biased questions: [   ]

Sampling Methods

In a [   ] sample, every member of the population has an [   ] chance of being selected.

In a [   ] sample, a [   ] is used to select members of the population.

In a [   ] sample, the population is divided into [   ] [   ]. Members are selected from each [   ].

In a [   ] sample, only members of the population who are [   ] are selected.

In a [   ] sample, members of the population can [   ] by volunteering.

Example 1 *Identifying Populations and Sampling Methods*

For each survey, describe the population and the sampling method.

a. A reporter wants to determine whether residents of your county agree or disagree with budget cuts that will close some branches of the public library. The reporter asks each customer at one branch of the public library whether they agree or disagree with the budget cuts.

b. A company wants to determine whether people who eat yogurt will like the company's new brand of yogurt. The company sends a researcher to a mall and the researcher asks for volunteers to participate in a taste test comparing the new brand of yogurt to other brands.

Solution

a. The population consists of [   ].
Because the reporter only asks customers at one library branch, the sample is a [   ] sample.

b. The population consists of [   ].
Because the researcher asks for volunteers, the sample is a [   ] sample.

✔ *Checkpoint*

1. A time management researcher wants to know if Americans feel that they have enough time to do what they want to do. The researcher goes to a shopping mall and asks the shoppers if they have enough time to do what they want to do. Describe the survey's population and sampling method.

Example 2   *Identifying Potentially Biased Samples*

Government A county council wants residents to give their opinions about a potential increase in property taxes. Residents can say either yes or no to the increase. The council needs the tax increase to keep every public library branch in the county open. Because the council cannot survey every resident, it decides to survey a sample. Tell whether the method could result in a biased sample. Explain.

> **County Council**
>
> Are you willing to pay more in property taxes to keep all county public library branches open?
>
> ☐ Yes
> ☐ No

a. Survey patrons at one of the library branches.

b. Give a phone number for county residents to call.

c. Visit a random sample of the county's residents at home and record their opinions.

Solution

a. This method could result in a [   ] sample because the library patrons have an interest in keeping the library open. They may favor an increase in taxes.

b. This method could result in a [   ] sample because the sample is [   ].

c. This method is less likely to result in a biased sample because a wide range of people will be surveyed. However, people who are not at home when the surveyor visits will not have their opinion recorded. As a result, the sample may be [   ].

✓ **Checkpoint**

2. Refer to the survey in Checkpoint 1. Do you think the survey could result in a biased sample? Explain.

Example 3 *Identifying Potentially Biased Questions*

Tell whether the question is potentially biased. Explain your answer. If the question is biased, rewrite it so that it is not.

a. Would you rather spend a lot of money watching a movie in a crowded movie theater or spend less money and watch a movie at home?

b. Don't you think that watching a football game is more interesting than watching a baseball game?

Solution

a. This question is [   ] because it suggests that watching a movie at home is better. An unbiased question is "[   ] [   ]?"

b. This question is [   ] because it suggests that watching a football game is more interesting. An unbiased question is "[   ]?"

✔ *Checkpoint* **Tell whether the question is potentially biased. Explain your answer. If the question is biased, rewrite it so that it is not.**

3. Do you agree with the unfair policy that requires students to wear uniforms to school?

4. Do you like the new frozen yogurt flavor?

Interpreting Data

Goal: Make conclusions about populations using surveys.

A margin of error accounts only for errors due to the nature of random sampling. It does not account for errors that result from biased questions or biased sampling.

Vocabulary

Margin of error:

Example 1   *Making a Population Prediction*

A tennis industry association wants to estimate the number of Americans 12 years old and older that played tennis at least 4 times in the last 12 months. The association conducts a survey of 1000 Americans 12 years old and older and finds that 62 of them played tennis at least 4 times in the past 12 months. Of all Americans 12 years old and older, estimate how many played tennis at least 4 times in the last 12 months. (There are about 237 million Americans 12 years old and older.)

Solution

To estimate the number of Americans 12 years old and older that played tennis at least 4 times in the past 12 months, follow these steps:

1. Find the percent of Americans in the sample that played tennis at least 4 times in the past 12 months.

   $$\boxed{} = \boxed{} = \boxed{} \%$$

2. Find $\boxed{}$% of the total number of Americans 12 years old and older.

   $$\boxed{}\% \cdot 237 \text{ million Americans} \approx \boxed{} \text{ Americans}$$

Answer: About $\boxed{}$ Americans 12 years old and older played tennis at least 4 times in the last 12 months.

Example 2   *Interpreting a Margin of Error*

Election A survey of a random sample of voters predicts that candidate A will receive 53% of the votes and that candidate B will receive 47% of the votes. The margin of error is ±4%. Can you predict who will win the election?

Solution

Use the margin of error to find intervals in which each candidate's actual percent is most likely to lie.

  Candidate A: 53% − 4% = ☐   53% + 4% = ☐

  Candidate B: 47% − 4% = ☐   47% + 4% = ☐

Using the margin of error, you can conclude that candidate A is likely to receive between ☐ and ☐ of the votes. Candidate B is likely to receive between ☐ and ☐ of the votes.

Answer: Because the intervals ☐ for the two candidates, you ☐ predict which candidate will win the election.

✔ *Checkpoint*

1. A survey of a random sample of voters predicts that candidate A will receive 54% of the votes and that candidate B will receive 46% of the votes. The margin of error is ±3%. Can you predict who will win the election?

Summary of Data Analysis

When reading the results of a survey, consider the following.

- Identify the population and the sampling method.

- Determine whether the [   ] represents the population.

- Determine whether the survey questions are [   ].

- Identify the margin of error.

- Determine whether any data displays are potentially [   ].

- Decide if the conclusions are supported by the [   ].

Example 3   Interpreting a Newspaper Survey

Tell what conclusions you can make from the following newspaper article.

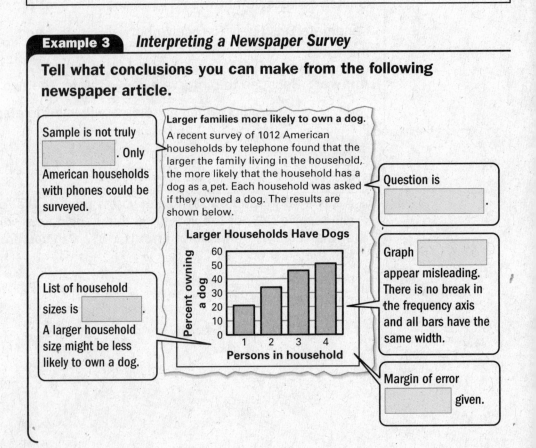

Sample is not truly [   ]. Only American households with phones could be surveyed.

Larger families more likely to own a dog.

A recent survey of 1012 American households by telephone found that the larger the family living in the household, the more likely that the household has a dog as a pet. Each household was asked if they owned a dog. The results are shown below.

Question is [   ].

Larger Households Have Dogs

List of household sizes is [   ]. A larger household size might be less likely to own a dog.

Graph [   ] appear misleading. There is no break in the frequency axis and all bars have the same width.

Margin of error [   ] given.

11.6 Permutations

Goal: Use permutations to count possibilities.

Vocabulary

Permutation:

n factorial:

0 factorial:

Example 1 *Counting Permutations*

Books You have 3 new books you want to read. In how many different orders can you read the books?

Solution

You have ☐ choices for the first book, ☐ choices for the second book, and ☐ choice for the third book. So, the number of orders you can read the books is ☐.

☐ = ☐ · ☐ · ☐ = ☐

Answer: You can read the books in ☐ different orders.

✓ **Checkpoint** Evaluate the factorial.

1. 4!	2. 0!	3. 5!	4. 6!

Permutations

Algebra The number of permutations of n objects taken r at a time can be written as $_nP_r$, where $_nP_r = \dfrac{n!}{(n-r)!}$.

Numbers $_5P_3 = \dfrac{5!}{(5-3)!} = \dfrac{5!}{2!} = \dfrac{5 \cdot 4 \cdot 3 \cdot \overset{1}{\cancel{2}} \cdot 1}{\underset{1}{\cancel{2}} \cdot 1} = \boxed{}$

Example 2 *Counting Permutations*

Marching Bands Judges at a marching band competition are awarding prizes to the first-, second-, third-, and fourth-place finishers. The competition has 12 marching bands. How many different ways can the first-, second-, third-, and fourth-place prizes be awarded?

Solution

To find the number of ways that prizes can be awarded, find $_{12}P_4$.

$_{12}P_4 = \boxed{}$ Use permutations formula.

$= \boxed{}$ Subtract.

$= \boxed{}$ Expand factorials. Divide out common factors.

$= \boxed{} \cdot \boxed{} \cdot \boxed{} \cdot \boxed{} = \boxed{}$ Multiply.

Answer: There are $\boxed{}$ ways the prizes can be awarded.

✔ **Checkpoint** Find the number of permutations.

5. $_8P_2$	6. $_5P_4$	7. $_7P_3$	8. $_4P_4$

Example 3   *Finding a Probability Using Permutations*

The combination for a lock consists of the numbers 3, 4, 6, and 8. You cannot remember the order in which the four numbers are to be entered. Find the probability that you open the lock on the first try.

Solution

Each possible combination is a permutation of the digits 3, 4, 6, and 8. The number of permutations of the four digits is ⬜.

$$\boxed{} = \boxed{} \cdot \boxed{} \cdot \boxed{} \cdot \boxed{} = \boxed{}$$

Only ⬜ of the possible permutations is correct, so the probability of opening the lock on the first try is ⬜.

✓ *Checkpoint*

9. Timothy created a password for his e-mail account by rearranging the letters of his name. You know how he created the password, but you do not know what the password is. What is the probability that you will guess the password on the first try?

10. A waitress takes ice cream cone orders for 5 people, but quickly forgets which person ordered which ice cream cone. If the waitress randomly chooses a person to give each ice cream cone to, what is the probability that the waitress will give the correct ice cream cone to each person?

Combinations

Goal: Use combinations to count possibilities.

Vocabulary

Combinations:

Example 1 *Listing Combinations*

You rent 3 movies to watch at home. You have enough time to watch 2 of the movies tonight. List and count the different possible pairs of movies you can watch tonight.

Solution

Use the letters A, B, and C to represent the 3 movies. List all possible pairs of movies. Then cross out any duplicates that represent the same pair of movies.

AB ☐

☐ ☐

☐ ☐

Answer: There are ☐ different pairs of movies.

✓ *Checkpoint* **Find the number of combinations.**

1. For a test, you can choose any 2 essay questions to answer from the 4 questions asked. How many different pairs of essay questions could you choose?

Combinations

Words To find the number of combinations of n objects taken r at a time, divide the number of permutations of n objects taken r at a time by $r!$.

Numbers $_9C_5 = \dfrac{_9P_5}{5!}$ **Algebra** $_nC_r = \dfrac{_nP_r}{r!}$

Example 2   *Counting Combinations*

Forming a Committee The manager of an accounting department wants to form a three-person advisory committee from the 10 employees in the department. How many different groups can the manager form?

Solution

The order in which the manager chooses people for the committee is not important. So, to find the number of different ways to choose 3 employees from 10, find $_{10}C_3$.

$_{10}C_3 = $ ⬜   Use combinations formula.

$= $ ⬜   Write ⬜ and ⬜ as products.

$= $ ⬜   Divide out common factors.

$= $ ⬜   Simplify.

Answer: There are ⬜ different groups the manager can form.

✔ *Checkpoint* **Find the number of combinations.**

2. $_5C_2$	**3.** $_9C_4$	**4.** $_6C_6$	**5.** $_{12}C_9$

Example 3   *Choosing Between Permutations and Combinations*

Tell whether the possibilities can be counted using *permutations* or *combinations*.

a. A survey asks people to rank comedy, drama, action, and science fiction according to how much they enjoy watching each type of movie. How many possible responses are there?

b. A literary magazine editor must choose 5 short stories for this month's issue from 30 submissions. How many different groups of 5 short stories can the editor choose?

Solution

a. Because the types of movies can be ranked first, second, third, or fourth, order is [   ]. So, the possibilities can be counted using [   ].

b. The order in which the editor chooses the short stories [   ] [   ] matter. So, the possibilities can be counted using [   ].

Example 4   *Finding a Probability Using Combinations*

A jury consists of 3 men and 9 women. Three jurors are selected at random for an interview. Find the probability that all 3 jurors chosen are men.

Solution

The order in which the jurors are chosen is not important. So, find $_{12}C_3$.

$$_{12}C_3 = \boxed{}$$ Use combinations formula.

$$= \boxed{}$$ Write $\boxed{}$ and $\boxed{}$ as products.

$$= \boxed{} = \boxed{}$$ Divide out common factors and simplify.

Answer: There are [   ] different combinations of 3 jurors that can be chosen for the interview. Only one of the combinations can have 3 men. So, the probability is [   ].

11.8 Probabilities of Disjoint and Overlapping Events

Goal: Find the probability that event A *or* event B occurs.

Vocabulary

Disjoint, or mutually exclusive, events:

Overlapping events:

Complementary events:

Example 1 *Identifying Disjoint and Overlapping Events*

Tell whether the events are *disjoint* or *overlapping*.

a. Roll a number cube.

 Event A: Roll an odd number.

 Event B: Roll a 3.

b. Randomly select a book.

 Event A: Select a fiction book.

 Event B: Select a math textbook.

Solution

a. The outcomes for event A are _____. The outcome

 for event B is 3. The events have _____ in common.

 Answer: The events are _____.

b. Because fiction books and math textbooks are not the same,
 there are _____ in common.

 Answer: The events are _____.

Probability of Disjoint Events

Words For two disjoint events, the probability that either of the events occurs is the sum of the probabilities of the events.

Algebra If A and B are disjoint events, then

$P(A \text{ or } B) = P(A) + P(B)$.

Example 2 *Finding the Probability of Disjoint Events*

Your school's varsity basketball team has 4 seniors, 5 juniors, and 3 sophomores. You randomly select 1 player to interview for the school newspaper. What is the probability that you select a sophomore or a junior?

Solution

The events are disjoint because a player cannot be both a sophomore and a junior.

Event A: Select a sophomore.

Event B: Select a junior.

$\quad P(A \text{ or } B) = P(A) + P(B)$ Probability of disjoint events

$\quad\quad\quad\quad = \boxed{} + \boxed{}$ Substitute probabilities.

$\quad\quad\quad\quad = \boxed{} = \boxed{}$ Add. Then simplify.

Answer: The probability that you select a sophomore or a junior is .

✔ **Checkpoint**

1. Refer to Example 2. What is the probability that you select a senior or a sophomore?

Probability of Overlapping Events

Words For two overlapping events, the probability that either of the events occurs is the sum of the probabilities of the events minus the probability of both events.

Algebra If A and B are overlapping events, then

$P(A \text{ or } B) = P(A) + P(B) - P(A \text{ and } B)$.

Example 3 *Finding the Probability of Overlapping Events*

You toss a quarter and a nickel. What is the probability that at least one of the coins shows tails?

Solution

The table lists all the possible outcomes of tossing two coins.

Event A: The quarter shows tails.

Event B: The nickel shows tails.

$P(A) = \boxed{}$

H, H	T, H
H, T	T, T

$P(B) = \boxed{}$ $P(A \text{ or } B) = \boxed{}$

$P(A \text{ or } B) = P(A) + P(B) - P(A \text{ and } B)$ Probability of overlapping events

$= \boxed{} + \boxed{} - \boxed{}$ Substitute probabilities.

$= \boxed{}$ Simplify.

Answer: The probability that at least one of the coins shows tails is $\boxed{}$.

Example 4   *Finding the Probability of Complementary Events*

Restaurant You and 8 friends are deciding where to go out for dinner. Each person's name is put in a hat. The person whose name is drawn picks the restaurant. What is the probability that your name is *not* chosen?

Solution

The events chosen and not chosen are ☐☐☐☐☐☐☐ events because one or the other must occur.

$$P(\text{not chosen}) = 1 - P(\text{chosen})$$ Probability of complementary events

$$= 1 - \boxed{}$$ Substitute for P(chosen).

$$= \boxed{}$$ Subtract.

Answer: The probability that your name is not chosen is $\boxed{}$.

✓ **Checkpoint**   Given $P(A)$, find $P(\text{not } A)$.

1. $P(A) = 24\%$	**2.** $P(A) = \dfrac{14}{37}$

11.9 Independent and Dependent Events

Goal: Find the probability that event A *and* event B occur.

Vocabulary

Independent events:

Dependent events:

Example 1   *Identifying Independent and Dependent Events*

Tell whether the events are *independent* or *dependent*.

a. In a class of 30 students, a gym teacher randomly chooses a student for a demonstration. From the remaining students, the teacher randomly chooses another student.

b. You roll a number cube. Then you roll the number cube again.

Solution

a. Because the teacher does not include the first student for the second selection, there is one fewer student to choose from. This affects the results of the second draw. So, the events are _____.

b. The result of the first roll does not affect the result of the second roll. So, the events are _____.

✓ Checkpoint

1. Tell whether the events are *independent* or *dependent*.

You randomly draw a numbered ball from a bowl. Then you put it back in the bowl and randomly draw another ball from the bowl.

> You can extend the formula for the probability of independent events to include more than two events. For example, the probability that independent events A, B, and C occur is the product $P(A) \cdot P(B) \cdot P(C)$.

Probability of Independent Events

Words For two independent events, the probability that both events occur is the product of the probabilities of the events.

Algebra If A and B are independent events, then

$P(A \text{ and } B) = P(A) \cdot P(B)$.

Example 2 *Finding the Probability of Independent Events*

States Each student in your class is to write a report on one of the first 13 states of the United States. Your teacher is allowing each state to be randomly chosen by more than one student. What is the probability that you and the student who sits next to you choose the same state?

Solution

Each state can be chosen more than once, so the choices are

[____] events. The probability of each event is [__].

$P(\text{state and same state}) = P(\text{state}) \cdot P(\text{same state})$

$= $ [__] $\cdot$ [__]

$= $ [__]

Answer: The probability that you both pick the same state is [__].

Probability of Dependent Events

Words For two dependent events, the probability that both events occur is the product of the probability that the first event occurs and the probability that the second event occurs given that the first event has occurred.

Algebra If A and B are dependent events, then

$P(A \text{ and } B) = P(A) \cdot P(B \text{ given } A)$.

Example 3 *Finding the Probability of Dependent Events*

In a box of 15 parts, 4 of the parts are defective. You randomly choose a part. Then you randomly draw a second part without replacing the first part. Find the probability that both parts are defective.

Solution

Because you don't replace the first part, the events are ⬚.
So, P(defective and then defective)
= P(defective) · P(defective given defective).

> Think: How many defective parts are remaining and how many total parts are remaining?

$P(\text{defective}) = \boxed{} \cdot$ There are ⬚ defective parts and ⬚ total parts.

$P(\text{defective given defective}) = \boxed{}$

$P(\text{defective and then defective}) = \boxed{} \cdot \boxed{}$ Substitute probabilities.

$= \boxed{} \approx \boxed{}$ Multiply. Write as a decimal.

Answer: The probability that both parts are defective is about ⬚%.

11 Words to Review

Give an example of the vocabulary word.

Stem-and-leaf plot

Frequency

Frequency table

Histogram

Box-and-whisker plot

Lower quartile

Upper quartile

Lower extreme

Upper extreme

Interquartile range

Categorical data

Numerical data

Population

Sample

Biased sample

Biased question

Margin of error

Permutation

n factorial

Combination

Disjoint events

Overlapping events

Dependent events

Independent events

Review your notes and Chapter 11 by using the Chapter Review on pages 640–643 of your textbook.

Polynomials

Goal: Classify and write polynomials in standard form.

Vocabulary

Polynomial:

Term:

Binomial:

Trinomial:

Degree of
a term:

Degree of a
polynomial:

Standard
form:

Example 1   *Identifying and Classifying Polynomials*

Tell whether the expression is a polynomial. If it is a polynomial,
list its terms and classify it.

a. $6ab$ **b.** $4t^2 - 8t - 5$ **c.** $-7y^{-3} + 1$

Solution

a. This expression is a polynomial. The only term is ☐ .
Because it has one term, it is a ☐ .

b. This expression is a polynomial. The terms are ☐ , ☐ ,
and ☐ . Because it has three terms, it is a ☐ .

c. This expression is not a polynomial. The variable y has an
exponent that is not a ☐ .

✓ Checkpoint Tell whether the expression is a polynomial.
If it is a polynomial, list its terms and classify it.

1. $9 + a^2 - 5a$	**2.** $-7 + 10m^3$
3. $-8p^2 - p - 6p^4 + p^{-3}$	

Example 2   *Finding the Degree of a Polynomial*

Find the degree of the polynomial.

a. **Polynomial:** $6w^4 - 3w + 7$

    Degree of term: ☐ ☐ ☐

The greatest degree of the terms is ☐. So, the degree of
$6w^4 - 3w + 7$ is ☐.

b. **Polynomial:** $a^2 + 5a^3b^3 - b$

    Degree of term: ☐ ☐ + ☐ = ☐ ☐

The greatest degree of the terms is ☐. So, the degree of
$a^2 + 5a^3b^3 - b$ is ☐.

Example 3   *Writing a Polynomial in Standard Form*

Write $-x^2 - 3(x - x^2) + 8x^3$ **as a polynomial in standard form.**

$-x^2 - 3(x - x^2) + 8x^3$

= ☐   Distributive property

= ☐   Write $-x^2$ as ☐x^2.

= ☐   Group like terms.

= ☐   Combine like terms.

= ☐   Standard form

✔ **Checkpoint** Find the degree of the polynomial.

4. $3g^3 + g - 6$	**5.** $-p^2 + 9p^5 + 7$	**6.** $r^2s - rs^3$

Write the expression as a polynomial in standard form.

7. $5x^2 + 2x^3 - 11$	**8.** $-d^2 + 4d^4 + 4d^2$

9. $3(7z - z^2) - 2(z + 5)$

Example 4 *Evaluating a Polynomial*

Ride You are on a freefall ride at an amusement park. The ride drops you from a height of 190 feet. Your height, in feet, after t seconds of falling, can be found using the polynomial $-16t^2 + 190$. Find your height after 3 seconds.

Solution

Evaluate the polynomial $-16t^2 + 190$ when $t = 3$.

$$-16t^2 + 190 = -16(\boxed{})^2 + 190 \qquad \text{Substitute for } t.$$

$$= -16(\boxed{}) + 190 \qquad \text{Evaluate the power.}$$

$$= \boxed{} + 190 \qquad \text{Multiply.}$$

$$= \boxed{} \qquad \text{Add.}$$

Answer: Your height after 3 seconds is $\boxed{}$.

✔ **Checkpoint** Evaluate the polynomial when $x = -2$ and $y = 4$.

10. $4x^2 + 2y - 5$	**11.** $-y^2 - 8x^3 + x$	**12.** $3xy^3 - x^2y$

12.2 Adding and Subtracting Polynomials

Goal: Add and subtract polynomials.

Example 1 *Adding Polynomials Vertically*

Find the sum.

a. $(5x^3 - x^2 + 6x - 4) + (7x^2 - 10x - 1)$

b. $(-x^4 - 4x^3 - 2x^2 - x - 3) + (2x^3 + 4x^2 + 5x - 2)$

Solution

a.
$$\boxed{}$$
$$+\ \boxed{}$$ Arrange like terms in columns.
$$\boxed{}$$ Add like terms.

b.
$$\boxed{}$$
$$+\ \boxed{}$$ Arrange like terms in columns.
$$\boxed{}$$ Add like terms.

Example 2 *Adding Polynomials Horizontally*

Find the sum.

a. $(-3y^2 - 8y + 1) + (-4y^2 + 12y - 2)$

b. $(4y^4 - 2y^3 + x^2 - 5x + 3) + (-x^3 + 6x^2 + 4)$

Solution

a. $(-3y^2 - 8y + 1) + (-4y^2 + 12y - 2)$

$= \boxed{}$ Group like terms.

$= \boxed{}$ Combine like terms.

b. $(4y^4 - 2y^3 + x^2 - 5x + 3) + (-y^3 + 6x^2 + 4)$

$= \boxed{}$ Group like terms.

$= \boxed{}$ Combine like terms.

Example 3   *Subtracting Polynomials Vertically*

Find the difference $(2x^2 - 9x - 5) - (4x^2 - 3x + 8).$

$$
\begin{array}{c}
2x^2 - 9x - 5 \\
-(4x^2 - 3x + 8) \\
\hline
\end{array}
\qquad\longrightarrow\qquad
\begin{array}{c}
2x^2 - 9x - 5 \\
+\left(\rule{12em}{0pt} \right) \\
\hline
\rule{12em}{0pt}
\end{array}
$$

Write opposite.

Add like terms.

Example 4   *Subtracting Polynomials Horizontally*

Find the difference $(3x^2 - 4x + 10) - (2x^2 - 7x + 9).$

$(3x^2 - 4x + 10) - (2x^2 - 7x + 9)$ Write difference.

$= 3x^2 - 4x + 10 + \left(\rule{10em}{0pt} \right)$ Write opposite of second polynomial.

$= \rule{12em}{0pt}$ Group like terms.

$= \rule{8em}{0pt}$ Combine like terms.

✓ *Checkpoint*   **Find the sum or difference.**

1. $(-2a^2 + 6a + 9) + (a^2 - 3a - 5)$

2. $(6y^2 - y) - (2y^2 + 5y + 9)$

3. $(3b^2 + 2b - 7) - (3b^2 + b - 4)$

4. $(-9m^3 - m^2 + m) - (m^3 - m^2)$

Goal: Multiply polynomials and monomials.

Example 1 *Multiplying a Monomial and a Binomial*

Find the product.

a. $4x(6x - 3)$ **b.** $(2c + 3)(-7c^2)$

Solution

a. $4x(6x - 3)$ Write product.

$= (\boxed{})6x - (\boxed{})3$ Distributive property

$= \boxed{}$ Product of powers property

b. $(2c + 3)(-7c^2)$ Write product.

$= 2c(\boxed{}) + 3(\boxed{})$ Distributive property

$= \boxed{}$ Product of powers property

Example 2 *Multiplying a Monomial and a Trinomial*

Find the product.

a. $y^2(8y^2 - 10y + 1)$ **b.** $(3m + 6mn - 2n)mn$

Solution

a. $y^2(8y^2 - 10y + 1)$ Write product.

$= (\boxed{})8y^2 - (\boxed{})10y + (\boxed{})1$ Distributive property

$= \boxed{}$ Product of powers property

b. $(3m + 6mn - 2n)mn$ Write product.

$= 3m(\boxed{}) + 6mn(\boxed{}) - 2n(\boxed{})$ Distributive property

$= \boxed{}$ Product of powers property

Example 3 *Dividing a Polynomial by a Monomial*

Find the quotient $\dfrac{-12x^6 + 15x^5 - 3x^3}{3x^3}$.

$$\dfrac{-12x^6 + 15x^5 - 3x^3}{3x^3}$$

$$= \dfrac{-12x^6}{\boxed{}} + \dfrac{15x^5}{\boxed{}} + \dfrac{-3x^3}{\boxed{}}$$ Rewrite quotient.

$$= \boxed{} + \boxed{} + \boxed{}$$ Divide numerators and denominators by $\boxed{}$.

$$= \boxed{}$$ Quotient of powers property

$$= \boxed{}$$ Simplify exponents.

$$= \boxed{}$$ Definition of zero exponent

✓ **Checkpoint** **Find the product or quotient.**

1. $-6n(2n - 1)$	**2.** $(-3b^2 + b - 7)(2b)$
3. $t^3(4t^2 - 3t + 8)$	**4.** $\dfrac{-4z^4 - 6z^3 + 7z^2}{-z^2}$

12.4 Multiplying Binomials

Goal: Multiply binomials.

Example 1 *Multiplying Binomials Using a Table*

Find the product $(4x + 1)(7x - 5)$.

Write any subtractions in the binomials as additions.

$(4x + 1)(7x - 5) = (4x + 1)[7x + (-5)]$

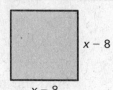

First binomial ⟶ ☐

Second binomial

	$7x$	☐
	☐	☐
1	$7x$	☐

The product is ☐, or ☐.

Example 2 *Using the Distributive Property*

Write an expression for the area of the square shown at the right. Then expand the expression and simplify.

$x - 8$

$x - 8$

Solution

> Use the formula for the area of a square: $A = s^2$.

An expression for the area of the square is $(x - 8)^2$. To expand the expression, multiply two binomials.

$(x - 8)^2 = (x - 8)(x - 8)$ Write two binomials.

$= \boxed{}(x - 8) - \boxed{}(x - 8)$ Distribute $\boxed{}$.

$= \boxed{} - \boxed{}$ Distribute $\boxed{}$ and $\boxed{}$.

$= \boxed{}$ Combine like terms.

Answer: The area is $\left(\boxed{}\right)$ square units.

Example 3 **Using the FOIL Method**

Find the product $(6x + 5)(-2x - 1)$.

First	+	Outer	+	Inner	+	Last
( )( )	+	( )( )	+	( )( )	+	( )( )

	+	( )	+	( )	+	( )

[ ]

✓ *Checkpoint* **Use a table to find the product.**

1. $(t + 4)(t + 8)$	**2.** $(m - 3)(m - 6)$	**3.** $(-5y + 1)(4y - 5)$

Find the product.

4. $(a + 2)(-3a + 2)$	**5.** $(p - 9)(p - 4)$	**6.** $(7n - 5)(2n + 5)$

Other Rules of Exponents

Goal: Simplify powers of products and quotients.

Rules of Exponents

Power of a Product Property

Words To find the power of a product, find the power of each factor and multiply.

Algebra $(ab)^m = \boxed{}$ **Numbers** $(3 \cdot 4)^2 = \boxed{}$

Power of a Quotient Property

Words To find the power of a quotient, find the power of the numerator and the power of the denominator and divide.

Algebra $\left(\dfrac{a}{b}\right)^m = \dfrac{\boxed{}}{\boxed{}}$, where $b \neq 0$ **Numbers** $\left(\dfrac{4}{7}\right)^5 = \dfrac{\boxed{}}{\boxed{}}$

Power of a Power Property

Words To find the power of a power, multiply the exponents.

Algebra $(a^m)^n = \boxed{}$ **Numbers** $(7^2)^3 = 7^{\boxed{}} = \boxed{}$

Example 1   *Finding Powers of Products*

a. $(3y)^2 = \boxed{} \cdot \boxed{}$ Power of a product property

$\qquad = \boxed{}$ Evaluate power.

b. $(-4b)^3 = \boxed{} \cdot \boxed{}$ Power of a product property

$\qquad = \boxed{}$ Evaluate power.

Example 2   *Finding Powers of Quotients*

Simplify the expression.

a. $\left(\dfrac{r}{s}\right)^8 = \dfrac{\boxed{}}{\boxed{}}$ Power of a quotient property

b. $\left(\dfrac{-5}{d}\right)^4 = \dfrac{\boxed{}}{\boxed{}}$ Power of a product property

$= \dfrac{\boxed{}}{\boxed{}}$ Evaluate power.

Example 3   *Finding a Power of a Power*

a. $(8^4)^4 = \boxed{}$ Power of a product property

b. $(a^6)^{-2} = \boxed{}$ Power of a product property

$= \dfrac{\boxed{}}{\boxed{}}$ Definition of a negative exponent

---

Example 4   *Using Properties of Exponents*

The side lengths of a square microchip are each 2.5×10^{-4} meter. What is the approximate area of the microchip?

Solution

To find the area of the microchip, use the formula for the area of a square.

$A = s^2$ Formula for area of a square

$= \left(\boxed{}\right)^2$ Substitute for s.

$= \left(\boxed{}\right)^2 \times \left(\boxed{}\right)^2$ Power of a product property

$= \left(\boxed{}\right)^2 \times \boxed{}$ Power of a power property

$= \boxed{} \times \boxed{}$ Evaluate power.

Answer: The microchip has an area of $\boxed{}$ square meter.

1. $(2z)^6$

2. $(-3q)^5$

3. $\left(\dfrac{c}{d}\right)^4$

4. $\left(\dfrac{-5}{g}\right)^3$

5. $(7^2)^3$

6. $(v^6)^{-5}$

7. $(5.4 \times 10^6)^2$

8. $(1.6 \times 10^{-8})^4$

Quadratic Functions

Goal: Graph quadratic functions.

Vocabulary

Quadratic function:	
Parabola:	
Nonlinear function:	
Minimum value:	
Maximum value:	

Example 1 *Evaluating a Quadratic Function*

To make a table of values for the quadratic function $y = x^2 + 4x + 2$, substitute several values of x into the equation. Then simplify to find the corresponding values for y.

x	Substitution	y
−4	$y = (\quad)^2 + 4(\quad) + 2$ $= \quad + (\quad) + 2$ $= \quad$	
−3	$y = (\quad)^2 + 4(\quad) + 2$	
−2	$y = (\quad)^2 + 4(\quad) + 2$	
−1	$y = (\quad)^2 + 4(\quad) + 2$	
0	$y = (\quad)^2 + 4(\quad) + 2$	

For $x = -4$, the process of substituting and simplifying is shown.

For $x = -3, -2, -1$, and 0, only substitution is shown.

Example 2 *Graphing a Quadratic Function*

Graph the function $y = 2x^2 - 5$.

1. Make a table of values. Choose several x-values and find the corresponding y-values.

x	−2	−1	0	1	2
y					

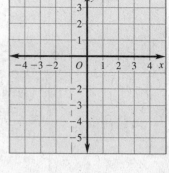

2. Use the table to make a list of ordered pairs.

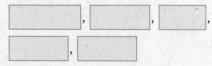

3. Graph the ordered pairs. Then draw a smooth curve through the points.

Example 3 *Graphing a Quadratic Function*

Graph the function $y = -\frac{1}{2}x^2 + 2x - 1$.

1. Make a table of values. Choose several x-values and find the corresponding y-values.

x	−2	0	2	4	6
y					

2. Use the table to make a list of ordered pairs.

3. Graph the ordered pairs. Then draw a smooth curve through the points.

Example 4 *Using a Calculator to Find a Maximum Value*

Rocket You launch a model rocket. The height of the rocket, in feet, is given by the equation $h = -16t^2 + 150t$, where t is the time in seconds after you launch the rocket. Find the greatest height reached by the rocket.

Solution

Use a graphing calculator to graph $h = -16t^2 + 150t$. Set the viewing window so that you can see the highest point on the graph. Using the calculator's *trace* feature, you can determine that the highest point on the graph is about $\left(\boxed{} , \boxed{} \right)$. So, the maximum value is about $\boxed{}$.

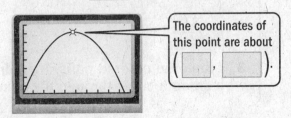

The coordinates of this point are about $\left(\boxed{} , \boxed{} \right)$.

Answer: The greatest height reached by the rocket is about $\boxed{}$ feet.

✔ **Checkpoint** **Make a table of values for the given function. Then graph the function.**

1. $x^2 - 4x + 1$

x					
y					

2. $-3x^2 - 6x + 2$

x					
y					

12.7 Exponential Growth and Decay

Goal: Graph exponential functions.

Vocabulary

Exponential function:

Exponential growth:

Exponential decay:

Example 1   *Graphing an Exponential Function*

Graph the exponential function $y = 2(3)^x$.

1. Make a table of values. Choose several x-values and find the corresponding y-values.

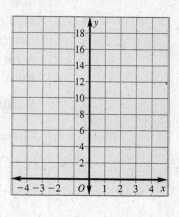

x	−3	−2	−1
y			

x	0	1	2
y			

2. Use the table to make a list of ordered pairs.

3. Graph the ordered pairs. Then draw a smooth curve through the points.

Example 2   *Graphing an Exponential Function*

Graph the exponential function $y = 5\left(\dfrac{1}{2}\right)^{x}$.

1. Make a table of values. Choose several x-values and find the corresponding y-values.

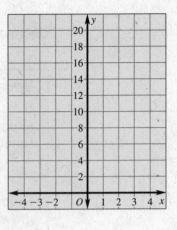

x	−2	−1	0
y			

x	1	2	3
y			

2. Use the table to make a list of ordered pairs.

3. Graph the ordered pairs. Then draw a smooth curve through the points.

Example 3   *Solving Problems Involving Exponential Decay*

In a factory, a piece of machinery that costs $45,000 depreciates at the rate of 20% per year. The machinery's value t years after purchase can be approximated by the function $V = 45{,}000(0.8)^{t}$. After how many years will the value of the machinery be less than $20,000?

Solution

Make a table of values for the function.

t	0	1	2	3	4
V					

Answer: After [ ] years the machinery will be worth less than $20,000.

Example 4   *Solving Problems Involving Exponential Growth*

A rancher begins his herd of Longhorn cattle with 20. The herd grows by about 30% per year. After how many years will the size of the herd triple?

Solution

Use a graphing calculator to graph the exponential function $P = \boxed{}\left(\boxed{}\right)^t$.

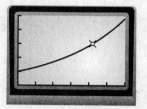

To estimate the value of t when $P = 3 \cdot 20 = 60,$ use the calculator's *trace* feature. You can determine that when $P = \boxed{}$, $t \approx \boxed{}$.

Answer: The herd population will triple after about $\boxed{}$ years.

✅ **Checkpoint**

1. Make a table of values for $y = 3(2)^x$. Then graph the function.

x	−3	−2	−1	0	1	2
y	$\boxed{}$	$\boxed{}$	$\boxed{}$	$\boxed{}$	$\boxed{}$	$\boxed{}$

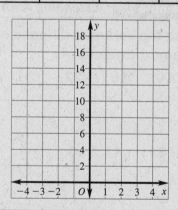

2. The function $A = 8000(0.95)^t$ gives the population of a town after t years. Tell whether this function is an example of exponential growth or decay. Explain your answer.

12.8 Sequences

Goal: Extend and graph sequences.

Vocabulary

Sequence:

Term:

Arithmetic sequence:

Common difference:

Geometric sequence:

Common ratio:

Example 1   *Extending Arithmetic Sequences*

Find the common difference for the arithmetic sequence. Then find the next three terms.

a. 10,   16,   22,   28,   34, . . .

[ ] [ ] [ ] [ ]

b. 8,   4,   0,   −4,   −8, . . .

[ ] [ ] [ ] [ ]

Solution

a. The common difference is [ ]. The next three terms in the sequence are [ ], [ ], and [ ].

b. The common difference is [ ]. The next three terms in the sequence are [ ], [ ], and [ ].

Example 2 *Extending Geometric Sequences*

Find the common ratio for the geometric sequence. Then find the next three terms.

a. 5,   15,   45,   135,   405, . . .

[ ] [ ] [ ] [ ]

b. 3,   −6,   12,   −24,   48, . . .

[ ] [ ] [ ] [ ]

Solution

a. The common ratio is [ ]. The next three terms in the sequence

are [ ] , [ ] , and [ ] .

b. The common ratio is [ ]. The next three terms in the sequence

are [ ] , [ ] , and [ ] .

✓ *Checkpoint* Tell whether the sequence is *arithmetic* or *geometric*. Then find the common difference or common ratio, and write the next three terms.

1. 10, 5, 0, −5, . . .	**2.** −4, 8, −16, 32, . . .

3. 240, 120, 60, 30, . . .

Example 3 — *Graphing an Arithmetic Sequence*

Graph the arithmetic sequence
4, 8, 12, 16, 20, ...

Write the sequence as a table of values.

Position number, x					
Term, y					

Then plot the points ( ), ( ), ( ), ( ), ( ).

Example 4 — *Graphing a Geometric Sequence*

Partition a square into four squares, as shown in Steps 1 and 2. Then partition each of the four squares into four squares. Continue partitioning the squares into four squares.

Write and graph a sequence for the number of new squares at each step.

Step 1   Step 2   Step 3   Step 4

The sequence 1, 4, 16, 64, . . . gives the number of squares at each step. Because each term is 4 times the previous term, the sequence is [ ].

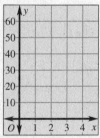

To graph the sequence, write the sequence as a table of values.

Position number, x				
Term, y				

Then plot the points ( ), ( ), ( ), ( ).

✔ *Checkpoint* **Write the next three terms of the sequence. Then graph the sequence.**

4. 1, 3, 9, 27, . . .

5. 24, 18, 12, 6, . . .

Give an example of the vocabulary word.

Polynomial	Term of a polynomial

Binomial	Trinomial

Degree of a term	Degree of a polynomial

Standard form	Quadratic function

Parabola

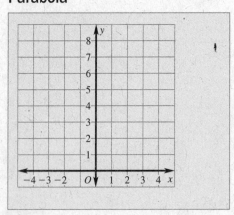

Nonlinear function

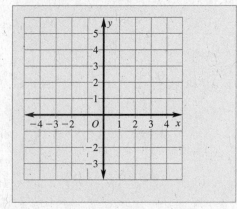

Minimum value of a function	Maximum value of a function

Exponential function

Exponential growth

Exponential decay

Sequence

Term (of sequence)

Arithmetic sequence

Common difference

Geometric sequence

Common ratio

Review your notes and Chapter 12 by using the Chapter Review on pages 698–701 of your textbook.

Angle Relationships

Goal: Classify special pairs of angles.

Vocabulary

Complementary
angles:

Supplementary
angles:

Vertical
angles:

Example 1 · *Identifying Complementary, Supplementary Angles*

In quadrilateral *PQRS*, identify all pairs of complementary angles
and supplementary angles.

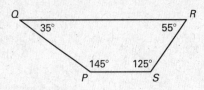

Solution

a. Because $m\angle Q + m\angle R = $ ☐ + ☐ = ☐ , $\angle Q$ and $\angle R$
are ☐ angles.

b. Because $m\angle P + m\angle Q = $ ☐ + ☐ = ☐ , $\angle P$ and $\angle Q$
are ☐ angles.

c. Because $m\angle R + m\angle S = $ ☐ + ☐ = ☐ , $\angle R$ and $\angle S$
are ☐ angles.

✓ Checkpoint Tell whether the angles are *complementary*, *supplementary*, or *neither*.

1. $m\angle1 = 37°$	**2.** $m\angle3 = 42°$	**3.** $m\angle5 = 127°$
$m\angle2 = 73°$	$m\angle4 = 48°$	$m\angle6 = 53°$

Example 2 *Finding an Angle Measure*

Adjacent angles that form a right angle are complementary. Adjacent angles that form a straight angle are supplementary.

For the diagram shown, $\angle1$ and $\angle2$ are complementary angles, and $m\angle1 = 46°$. Find $m\angle2$.

Solution

$m\angle1 + m\angle2 = \boxed{}$ Definition of complementary angles

$\boxed{} + m\angle2 = \boxed{}$ Substitute for $m\angle1$.

$m\angle2 = \boxed{}$ Subtract $\boxed{}$ from each side.

✓ Checkpoint $\angle1$ and $\angle2$ are complementary angles. Given $m\angle1$, find $m\angle2$.

4. $m\angle1 = 64°$	**5.** $m\angle1 = 13°$
6. $m\angle1 = 82°$	**7.** $m\angle1 = 7°$

Example 3   *Using Supplementary and Vertical Angles*

For the diagram shown, $m\angle 1 = 65°$.
Find $m\angle 2$, $m\angle 3$, and $m\angle 4$.

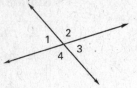

Solution

a. $m\angle 1 + m\angle 2 = \boxed{}$ $\angle 1$ and $\angle 2$ are supplementary.

   $\boxed{} + m\angle 2 = \boxed{}$ Substitute for $m\angle 1$.

   $m\angle 2 = \boxed{}$ Subtract $\boxed{}$ from each side.

b. $m\angle 3 = \boxed{}$ Vertical angles have same measure.

   $m\angle 3 = \boxed{}$ Substitute for $m\angle 1$.

c. $m\angle 4 = \boxed{}$ Vertical angles have same measure.

   $m\angle 4 = \boxed{}$ Substitute for $m\angle 2$.

✔ *Checkpoint*

8. $\angle 1$ and $\angle 2$ are supplementary angles, and $m\angle 1 = 132°$. Find $m\angle 2$.

9. $\angle 3$ and $\angle 4$ are supplementary angles, and $m\angle 3 = 23°$. Find $m\angle 4$.

10. In Example 3, suppose that $m\angle 1 = 54°$. Find $m\angle 2$, $m\angle 3$, and $m\angle 4$.

13.2 Angles and Parallel Lines

Goal: Identify angles when a transversal intersects lines.

Vocabulary

Transversal:

Corresponding angles:

Alternate interior angles:

Alternate exterior angles:

Example 1 *Identifying Angles*

In the diagram, line *t* is a transversal. Tell whether the angles are *corresponding*, *alternate interior*, or *alternate exterior* angles.

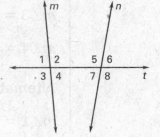

a. ∠1 and ∠5

b. ∠2 and ∠7

c. ∠3 and ∠6

Solution

a. ∠1 and ∠5 are   angles.

b. ∠2 and ∠7 are   angles.

c. ∠3 and ∠6 are   angles.

✓ *Checkpoint* In Example 1, tell whether the angles are corresponding, *alternate interior*, or *alternate exterior* angles.

1. ∠4 and ∠5	**2.** ∠1 and ∠8	**3.** ∠4 and ∠8

Angles and Parallel Lines

In the diagram, transversal *t* intersects parallel lines *m* and *n*.

Corresponding angles

m∠1 = [ ]

m∠2 = [ ]

m∠3 = [ ]

m∠4 = [ ]

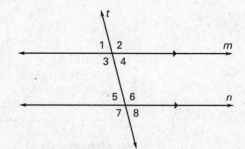

Alternate interior angles

m∠3 = [ ]

m∠4 = [ ]

Alternate exterior angles

m∠1 = [ ]

m∠2 = [ ]

Example 2 *Finding Angle Measures*

In the diagram, transversal *t* intersects parallel lines *m* and *n*. If $m\angle 1 = 100°$, find the measures of the other numbered angles.

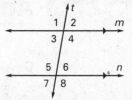

Solution

$m\angle 5 =$ ☐ , because $\angle 1$ and $\angle 5$ are ☐ angles.

$m\angle 4 =$ ☐ , because $\angle 4$ and $\angle 5$ are ☐ angles.

$m\angle 8 =$ ☐ , because $\angle 1$ and $\angle 8$ are ☐ angles.

$m\angle 2 =$ ☐ , because $\angle 1$ and $\angle 2$ are ☐ angles.

$m\angle 6 =$ ☐ , because $\angle 2$ and $\angle 6$ are ☐ angles.

$m\angle 3 =$ ☐ , because $\angle 3$ and $\angle 6$ are ☐ angles.

$m\angle 7 =$ ☐ , because $\angle 2$ and $\angle 7$ are ☐ angles.

✓ **Checkpoint**

4. In Example 2, if $m\angle 2 = 85°$, find the measures of the other angles.

Example 3 *Finding the Value of a Variable*

If a transversal intersects two lines so that the corresponding angles have the same measure, then the lines are parallel.

Find the value of *x* that makes lines *m* and *n* parallel.

Solution

The labeled angles in the diagram are corresponding angles. Lines *m* and *n* are ☐ when the measures are ☐ .

☐ = ☐ Set measures equal.

☐ = ☐ Subtract ☐ from each side.

$x =$ ☐ Divide each side by ☐ .

13.3 Angles and Polygons

Goal: Find measures of interior and exterior angles.

Vocabulary

Interior
angle:

Exterior
angle:

Measures of Interior Angles of a Convex Polygon

The sum of the measures of the interior angles of a convex n-gon is given by the formula $(n-2) \cdot 180°$.

The measure of an interior angle of a regular n-gon is given by the formula $\dfrac{(n-2) \cdot 180°}{n}$.

Example 1   *Finding the Sum of a Polygon's Interior Angles*

Find the sum of the measures of the interior angles of the polygon.

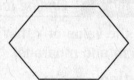

Solution

For a convex hexagon, $n = \boxed{}$.

$$(n-2) \cdot 180° = \left(\boxed{} - 2\right) \cdot 180°$$

$$= \boxed{} \cdot 180°$$

$$= \boxed{}$$

Example 2 *Finding the Measure of an Interior Angle*

Find the measure of an interior angle of a regular octagon.

Solution

For a regular octagon, $n = 8$.

Measure of an interior angle = [   ]   Write formula.

= [   ]   Substitute for n.

= [   ]   Simplify.

✓ *Checkpoint*

1. Find the sum of the measures of the interior angles of a convex 9-gon.

2. Find the measure of an interior angle of a regular 18-gon.

Example 3 *Finding the Measure of an Exterior Angle*

An interior angle and an exterior angle at the same vertex form a straight angle.

Find $m\angle 1$ in the diagram.

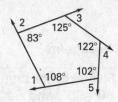

Solution

The angle that measures [   ] forms a straight angle with $\angle 1$, which is the exterior angle at the same vertex.

$m\angle 1 + $ [   ] $= $ [   ]   Angles are supplementary.

$m\angle 1 = $ [   ]   Subtract [   ] from each side.

3. In Example 3, find $m\angle 2$, $m\angle 3$, $m\angle 4$, and $m\angle 5$.

Example 4 *Using the Sum of Measures of Exterior Angles*

> Each vertex of a convex polygon has two exterior angles. If you draw one exterior angle at each vertex, then the sum of the measures of these angles is 360°.

Find the unknown angle measure in the diagram.

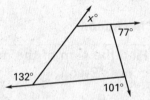

Solution

$x° + 77° + 101° + 132° = \boxed{}$ Sum of measures of exterior angles of a convex polygon is 360°.

$x + \boxed{} = \boxed{}$ Add.

$x = \boxed{}$ Subtract $\boxed{}$ from each side.

Answer: The angle measure is $\boxed{}$.

✔ **Checkpoint**

4. Five exterior angles of a convex hexagon have measures 42°, 78°, 60°, 55°, and 62°. Find the measure of the sixth exterior angle.

13.4 Translations

Goal: Translate figures in a coordinate plane.

Vocabulary

Transformation:

Image:

Translation:

Tessellation:

Example 1 **Describing a Translation**

> In a translation, a figure and its image are congruent.

For the diagram shown, describe the translation in words.

Solution

Think of moving horizontally and vertically from a point on the original figure to the corresponding point on the new figure. For instance, you move [ ] units to the [ ] and [ ] units [ ] from $A(-3, -2)$ to reach A' [ ].

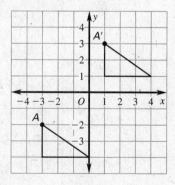

Coordinate Notation

You can describe a translation of each point (x, y) of a figure using the coordinate notation

$$(x, y) \rightarrow (x + a, y + b)$$

where a indicates how many units a point moves horizontally, and b indicates how many units a point moves [____]. Move the point (x, y) to the right if a is positive and to the [___] if a is [_____]. Move the point up if b is positive and [_____] if b is [_____].

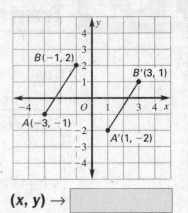

$(x, y) \rightarrow$ [_____]

Example 2 *Translating a Figure*

Draw $\triangle ABC$ with vertices $A(-2, 1)$, $B(-1, 4)$, and $C(0, 1)$. Then find the coordinates of the vertices of the image after the translation $(x, y) \rightarrow (x + 4, y - 5)$, and draw the image.

Solution

First draw $\triangle ABC$. Then, to translate $\triangle ABC$, [_____] to the x-coordinate and [_____] from the y-coordinate of each vertex.

Original		Image
(x, y)	$\rightarrow$	$(x + 4, y - 5)$
$A(-2, 1)$	$\rightarrow$	A' [_____]
$B(-1, 4)$	$\rightarrow$	B' [_____]
$C(0, 1)$	$\rightarrow$	C' [_____]

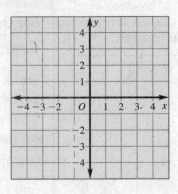

Finally, draw $\triangle A'B'C'$. Notice that each point on $\triangle ABC$ moves [__] units to the [_____] and [__] units [_____].

1. Draw quadrilateral *PQRS* with vertices $P(-4, -1)$, $Q(-1, 0)$, $R(-2, -3)$, and $S(-4, -4)$. Then find the coordinates of the image after the translation $(x, y) \rightarrow (x + 6, y + 5)$, and draw the image.

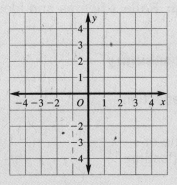

Example 3 *Creating Tessellations*

Tell whether you can create a tessellation using only translations of the given polygon. If you can, create a tessellation. If not, explain why not.

a.

b.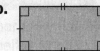

Solution

a. You [ ] translate a regular octagon to create a tessellation. Notice in the design that there [ ] gaps and overlaps.

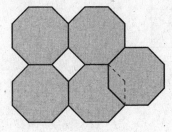

b. You [ ] translate the rectangle to create a tessellation. Notice in the design that there [ ] gaps or overlaps.

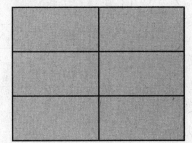

13.5 Reflections and Symmetry

Goal: Reflect figures and identify lines of symmetry.

Vocabulary

Reflection:

Line of reflection:

Line symmetry:

Line of symmetry:

Example 1   *Identifying Reflections*

> In a reflection, a figure and its image are congruent.

Tell whether the transformation is a reflection. If so, identify the line of reflection.

a. 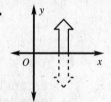   b. 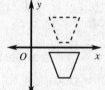   c.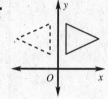

Solution

a.

b.

c.

Coordinate Notation

You can use coordinate notation to describe the images of figures after reflections in the axes of a coordinate plane.

Reflection in the x-axis

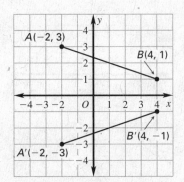

Multiply the y-coordinate by −1.

$(x, y) \rightarrow$ ☐

Reflection in the y-axis

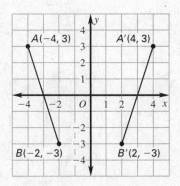

Multiply the x-coordinate by −1.

$(x, y) \rightarrow$ ☐

Example 2   *Reflecting a Triangle*

Draw △ABC with vertices A(2, 2), B(2, 5), and C(4, 1). Then find the coordinates of the vertices of the image after a reflection in the x-axis, and draw the image.

Solution

First draw △ABC. Then, to reflect △ABC in the x-axis, multiply the y-coordinate of each vertex by ☐.

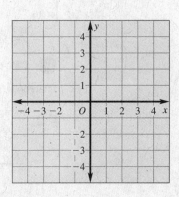

Original		Image
(x, y)	→	☐
A(2, 2)	→	A′ ☐
B(2, 5)	→	B′ ☐
C(4, 1)	→	C′ ☐

Finally, draw △A′B′C′.

✔ **Checkpoint**

1. Draw △*ABC* with vertices *A*(−4, −3), *B*(−4, 4), and *C*(−1, −3). Then find the coordinates of the vertices of the image of △*ABC* after a reflection in the *y*-axis, and draw the image.

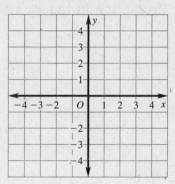

Example 3   *Identifying Lines of Symmetry*

Draw the lines of symmetry on the figure. Tell how many lines of symmetry the figure has.

a.

b.

c.

✔ **Checkpoint**   Draw the lines of symmetry on the figure. Tell how many lines of symmetry the figure has.

2.

3.

4.

13.6 Rotations and Symmetry

Goal: Rotate figures and identify rotational symmetry.

Vocabulary

Rotation:

Center of rotation:

Angle of rotation:

Rotational symmetry:

Example 1 *Identifying Rotations*

> In a rotation, a figure and its image are congruent.

Tell whether the transformation is a rotation about the origin. If so, give the angle and direction of the rotation.

a. 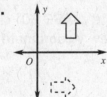   b. 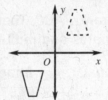   c.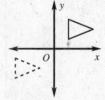

Solution

a.

b.

c.

90° Rotations

In this lesson, all rotations in the coordinate plane are centered at the origin. You can use coordinate notation to describe a 90° rotation of a figure about the origin.

90° clockwise rotation

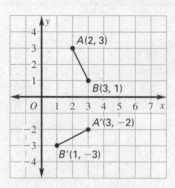

90° counterclockwise rotation

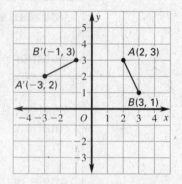

Switch the coordinates, then multiply the new y-coordinate by -1.

$(x, y) \rightarrow$ ⬜

Switch the coordinates, then multiply the new x-coordinate by -1.

$(x, y) \rightarrow$ ⬜

Example 2   *Rotating a Triangle*

Draw $\triangle ABC$ with vertices $A(1, 1)$, $B(3, 4)$, and $C(4, 0)$. Then find the coordinates of the vertices of the image after a 90° clockwise rotation, and draw the image.

Solution

First draw $\triangle ABC$. Then, to rotate $\triangle ABC$ 90° clockwise, switch the coordinates and multiply the new y-coordinate by -1.

Original		Image
(x, y)	$\rightarrow$	⬜
$A(1, 1)$	$\rightarrow$	A' ⬜
$B(3, 4)$	$\rightarrow$	B' ⬜
$C(4, 0)$	$\rightarrow$	C' ⬜

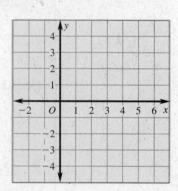

Finally, draw $\triangle A'B'C'$.

✔ *Checkpoint*

1. Draw △*ABC* with vertices *A*(1, −1), *B*(3, −1), and *C*(4, −4). Then find the coordinates of the vertices of the image after a 90° counterclockwise rotation, and draw the image.

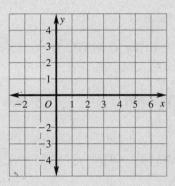

180° Rotations

To rotate a point 180° about the origin, multiply each coordinate by −1. The image is the same whether you rotate the figure

[   ] or [   ].

(x, y) → [   ]

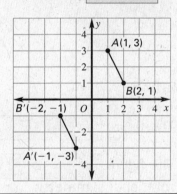

Example 3   *Rotating a Triangle*

Draw △*MNP* with vertices *M*(−4, −4), *N*(−3, −1), and *P*(−1, −2). Then find the coordinates of the vertices of the image after a 180° rotation, and draw the image.

Solution

First draw △*MNP*. Then, to rotate △*MNP* 180°, multiply the coordinates by −1.

Original		Image
(*x*, *y*)	→	
M(−4, −4)	→	*M*′
N(−3, −1)	→	*N*′
P(−1, −2)	→	*P*′

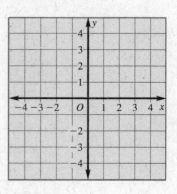

Finally, draw △*M*′*N*′*P*′.

Example 4   *Identifying Rotational Symmetry*

Tell whether the figure has rotational symmetry. If so, give the angle and direction of rotation.

a.    b.   c.

Solution

a. The figure [ ] rotational symmetry.

b. The figure [ ] rotational symmetry.

c. The figure [ ] [ ] rotational symmetry.

Dilations

Goal: Dilate figures in a coordinate plane.

Vocabulary

Dilation:

Center of dilation:

Scale factor:

Dilation

> In a dilation, a figure and its image are similar.

In this lesson, the origin of the coordinate plane is the center of dilation.

In the diagram, $\overline{A'B'}$ is the image of $\overline{AB}$ after a dilation. Because $\dfrac{A'B'}{AB} = 2$, the scale factor is [ ]. You can describe a dilation with respect to the origin using the notation

$$(x, y) \rightarrow (kx, ky)$$

where k is the [ ].

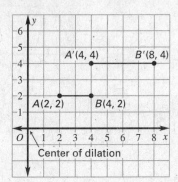

Example 1   *Dilating a Quadrilateral*

Draw quadrilateral with vertices $A(-4, 1)$, $B(1, 3)$, $C(1, -1)$, and $D(-3, -1)$. Then find the coordinates of the vertices of the image after a dilation having a scale factor of 2, and draw the image.

Solution

First draw quadrilateral *ABCD*. Then, to dilate *ABCD*, multiply the *x*- and *y*-coordinates of each vertex by ☐ .

Original		Image
(x, y)	→	☐
$A(-4, 1)$	→	A' ☐
$B(1, 3)$	→	B' ☐
$C(1, -1)$	→	C' ☐
$D(-3, -1)$	→	D' ☐

> Notice in Example 1 that when $k > 1$, the new figure is an enlargement of the original figure.

Finally, draw quadrilateral $A'B'C'D'$.

✔ **Checkpoint**

1. Draw $\triangle DEF$ with vertices $D(-3, 2)$, $E(1, 2)$, and $F(1, -1)$. Then find the coordinates of the vertices of the image after a dilation having a scale factor of 3, and draw the image.

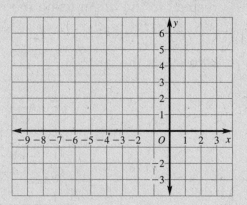

Example 2   *Using a Scale Factor Less than 1*

Draw △*PQR* with vertices *P*(−8, 4), *Q*(−6, 6), and *R*(−4, −2). Then find the coordinates of the vertices of the image after a dilation having a scale factor of 0.5, and draw the image.

Solution

Draw △*PQR*. Then, to dilate △*PQR*, multiply the *x*- and *y*-coordinates of each vertex by [ ].

Original		Image
(*x*, *y*)	→	[ ]
P(−8, 4)	→	*P*′ [ ]
Q(−6, 6)	→	*Q*′ [ ]
R(−4, −2)	→	*R*′ [ ]

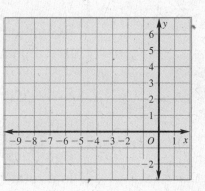

Finally, draw △*P*′*Q*′*R*′.

> Notice in Example 2 that when *k* < 1, the new figure is a reduction of the original figure.

Example 3   *Finding a Scale Factor*

Computer Graphics An artist uses a computer program to enlarge a design, as shown. What is the scale factor of the dilation?

Solution

The width of the original design is [ ] = [ ] units. The width of the image is [ ] = [ ] units. So, the scale factor is $\dfrac{[\ ]\text{ units}}{[\ ]\text{ units}}$, or [ ].

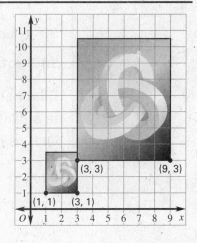

✔ *Checkpoint*

2. Given $\overline{CD}$ with endpoints *C*(6, −9) and *D*(−3, 1), let $\overline{C'D'}$ with endpoints *C*′(2, −3) and $D'\left(-1, \dfrac{1}{3}\right)$ be the image of $\overline{CD}$ after a dilation. Find the scale factor.

Summary
Transformations in a Coordinate Plane

Translations

In a translation, each point of a figure is moved
the [_____] in the [_____].

$(x, y) \rightarrow$ [_____]

Reflections

In a reflection, a figure is [_____] over a line.

Reflection in x-axis: $(x, y) \rightarrow$ [_____]

Reflection in y-axis (shown): $(x, y) \rightarrow$ [_____]

Rotations

In a rotation, a figure is turned about the origin
through a given [_____] and [_____].

90° clockwise rotation (shown): $(x, y) \rightarrow$ [_____]

90° counterclockwise rotation: $(x, y) \rightarrow$ [_____]

180° rotation: $(x, y) \rightarrow$ [_____]

Dilations

In a dilation, a figure [_____] or [_____]
with respect to the origin.

$(x, y) \rightarrow$ [_____] , where k is the [_____].

Words to Review

Give an example of the vocabulary word.

Complementary angles

Supplementary angles

Vertical angles

Transversal

Corresponding angles

Alternate interior angles

Alternate exterior angles

Interior angle

Exterior angle

Transformation

Image

Translation

Tessellation

Reflection, line of reflection

Line symmetry, line of symmetry

Rotational symmetry

Rotation, center of rotation, angle of rotation

Dilation, center of dilation, scale factor

Review your notes and Chapter 13 by using the Chapter Review on pages 752–755 of your textbook.